Virtual Tour Photography for Real Estate

How to create professional 360 tours

By: Nathan Cool

To Jack, from "Ampa"

Table of Contents

Table of Contents 5

Introduction 9

Safety First 13

Virtual Tour Basics 15
    360 vs. 3D 15
    360° Photography Overview 16
    The Steps Involved 20
    Nadirs and Zeniths 21

Gear..23
    Portable 360° Camera Gear 23
        Ricoh Thetas 23
        QooCam 8K 25
        Insta360 One X and One R 26
        Stands 27
        Cases 29
        Remote Control 30
    DSLR Gear 31
        Camera Body 32
        Fisheye Lens 33
        Pano Head 33
        Tripod 34
        Lights/Flash 35
        Flash Trigger 36
            White Balance Issues with Triggers 37
        Remote Control 38
    The Hybrid Approach 39
    Pro 360 Cameras 40

Hosting Services 41
    CloudPano 41
    Marzipano (self-hosting) 42
    Tourweaver (self-hosting) 43

Kuula..44
Cupix...44
Matterport 45
EyeSpy360..47
Ricoh Tours 47

Photographing a 360 49
Compositions 50
Camera Height 51
Initial View Optimization 52
Lens Direction.............................55
Room Perspectives.........................56
Room Navigations 58
Room Transitions..........................58
Portable 360 Cameras 60
Exposure Settings (Exteriors) 61
Exposure Settings (Interiors) 62
DSLRs..64
Camera Mounting 65
Initial Setup (parallax calibration) 67
Footage Overview............................74
Shooting Exterior Footage 78
Shooting Interiors with no Flash..........82
Shooting Interiors with Flash.............83
Prepare your flash 85
Level your tripod........................85
Set your focus...........................85
Find the starting angle.................86
Set the white balance...................87
Determine your exposure settings........88
Shoot the rotational shots..............89
Shoot the zenith........................91
Shooting the Nadir (optional) 92

Using Flash 95
The Principles for Flash.......................95
Flash Gear......................................98
Flash Position..................................99
Window Pulls....................................99

Flash-Ambient Blending.................................100
   Example 101

Software 105
   Lightroom and Photoshop..........................105
   Stitchers for Portable Cameras 106
      Ricoh..106
      QooCam 110
      Insta360...114
   Stitchers for DSLRs 114
      PTGui...115
      Panoweaver 115
      Hugin...117

Editing Workflows.....................................119
   Portable Camera Workflows.....................119
      The Quick and Dirty 120
      Exposure Blending...........................120
      Photoshop Edits 129
         Remove camera from mirrors 129
         Color Layers................................129
         Selective White Balance 132
         Desaturate Ceilings 133
      Stitching 135
      Workflow Steps 135
         Ricoh Theta Z1..........................136
         QooCam 8K 140
         Insta360 One X 142
      Nadir Patching 143
   DSLR Workflow....................................144
      Nadir Patching 149

PTGui Primer..155
   Basic Stitching......................................155
   Control Points 159
   Output 164

Hosting..165
   Uploading 165

Setting the Initial View 167
Adding Navigation 167
Publishing 169
Embedding 169

Pricing 171

Further Reading 177

Lightroom Presets 181
Portable 360 Cameras 181
360 Import 181
360 Full Bump 182
DSLR 183
Import 183
Interior 183
Exterior 184

Introduction

Covid-19 changed the world of real estate photography — forever. With health concerns being a market driver for distance-solutions, many realtors are now opting for add-ons to provide remote, virtual experiences. This isn't a short-term fad. Virtual solutions are a trend that, while actually getting underway before the pandemic, will very likely continue for quite some time as "new normals" are evolving into *de facto* ways of doing business in real estate, while influencing buyer- and seller-psychology. This has become evident with not only increased workloads for many real estate photographers, but also the availability of gear flying off shelves to create virtual tours for real estate listings. While virtual tours — *real* 360° user-controlled navigable tours, not slideshows of pictures — may have been less popular among many realtors in the past, they are now in the forefront, and with staying power.

Oftentimes things start for one reason and then continue for others. In the case of virtual tours, the convenience of walking through homes without having to physically drive to them has more than a just a short-term, pandemic-proof appeal. Virtual tours have an added side-effect of expectation: sellers and buyers are — and will continue to be — expecting a property to have a virtual experience. Even before the Covid-19 pandemic this trend was taking off, which was something I reported on in late 2019[1] when I discussed survey results from the National Association of Realtors showing virtual tours being one of the top website features buyers found useful. That was pre-Covid. The pandemic escalated that need. While it could be argued that buyers will no doubt *eventually* want to physically visit properties, during their initial winnowing-out phase virtual tours provide a tool that can help buyers make a more informed decision than pictures alone. This provides lasting-power to virtual tours, and a major reason it will likely become more popular than it was in the past. So if you've considered

---

[1] See https://youtu.be/omgcRgr5v94

expanding your real estate photography business, virtual tours may now be an option to pursue. That's where this book comes in.

This seventh book in my real estate photography series is a guide to creating virtual tours for real estate by photographing, editing, and hosting 360° panoramic virtual tours, covering a broad range starting with simple portable cameras, progressing through the high-end results by using DSLRs with flash (and methods in between).

The print version of this book doesn't have all the bells and whistles of an e-book. It also costs more to print (especially when including color images) hence the higher price than my e-books. But, I do understand the advantages of having this print copy. Yet, being a physical book, there are limitations including:

1. No hyperlinks. In my e-books you can quickly jump between sections, and to external resources such as my video tutorials, product pages, etc. While an e-book is more interactive, I've included links wherever I could in this print version, but it does require of course that you type those into a web browser, versus just clicking on them in an e-book.

2. Lower image quality. In my e-books, all of the images, screen shots, etc., are in high-res, allowing you to zoom in on the images to see all the details, full screen. Annotated screen shots and images in this printed book may be hard to see compared to using the e-book. When possible, I cropped images down for this print edition so that only relevant portions were shown. In some cases, I dedicated an entire page to an image, rotated to a landscape layout to make the image more readable.

Nevertheless, this paperback version has the same information and pictures — it just doesn't provide the niceties that the e-books provide.

I'll start by covering safety, which is paramount. DO NOT SKIP THIS CHAPTER! After covering these safety protocols, I'll discuss the basics of this type of photography, and then jump right into the gear to use. Hosting services/solutions are necessary for displaying your tours, which is covered next, before going through the steps to shoot and edit the footage you'll upload to these hosts, and how you might charge for your services.

If any of this so far has your mind filled with question marks, not to worry; this may be simpler than you think. But, depending on the various route you take, you may find that what might appear like the shortest path to success could have many more bumps along the way. Namely, it's become popular to use inexpensive, portable 360 cameras, yet not all are created equal, nor are they "naturally" up to the task for professional use. Thus, it's important to cover the other end of the spectrum: going high-end using DSLRs combined with lighting to achieve very impressive 360° virtual tours. I'll cover both sides (and options in between) and I'll ask that you consider both approaches since being skilled at more than one method could get you more work, more clients, and never limit what you can produce, and achieve.

If producing 360° virtual tours may be new to you and its terms and processes different than what you're accustomed to, remember that it's only that: New. If you're already shooting real estate photography (or similar genre) then most of the effort is behind you, and you are just a few steps away from producing impressive 360° virtual tours. But, there are prerequisites for this book.

To keep this book as streamlined as possible, I've written it with the assumption that you know how to use at least the basics of Adobe's Lightroom and Photoshop. Specifically, it will be very important that you're familiar with the techniques in my interiors book, and to some degree working with Photoshop layers like I discuss in my advanced editing book. The other books in my real estate photography series aren't required, but you may find them useful subject matter, in particular my book on business techniques, as many of the principles there apply to providing virtual tours as well.

Along with the books in my real estate photography series, I also provide free online tutorials on my YouTube channel at:

https://www.youtube.com/c/NathanCoolPhoto

Subscribing to my YouTube channel is free, and as new videos get posted you'll be notified. It's a great way to see firsthand techniques while staying on top of some of the latest ways to improve your photography skills and business.

I also post tips, info, recent work, and various photography tidbits on my Facebook and Instagram pages, which you can follow at:

https://www.facebook.com/NathanCoolPhoto

and

https://www.instagram.com/nathancool

If all else fails and you get stuck, I also offer limited, remote, one-on-one photography coaching for real estate photographers around the world, where I can guide you through issues via web conference with screen sharing. If you get to a point where you think a private session with me would be useful, you can email me for more information on price and availability at Nathan@NathanCoolPhoto.com

And now without further ado, let's begin.

Safety First

Before getting started it's of the utmost importance that you ensure your safety and the safety of those you may come in contact with when working in the field creating virtual tours. While the recent pandemic has been a market-driver for virtual tours, it doesn't mean this comes without risk. The new normals and de facto ways of conducting real estate business are changing, and safety protocols are in place through many agencies and realtor boards.[2] I spoke about this some time back[3], and those practices (as well as others) continue to be recommended. In this short yet highly important chapter, I want to quickly cover safety items that go beyond the security issues I talk about in my business techniques book to address additional steps I recommend be taken by real estate photographers, including those wanting to capture virtual tours.

Disclaimer: You should ensure that all safety protocols you follow are in accordance with federal, state, and local requirements, as well as those imposed by any realty agencies, MLSs, or realtor boards in your area.

With that said, here are points of protocol I recommend you take, as a minimum:

1. If anyone residing at the property has tested positive for Covid-19 or is otherwise self-quarantined, do not enter the property. Cancel this job. Otherwise, continue.

2. All persons must vacate the property at least one hour prior to the photographer's arrival and not return until the photographer has left the property.

---

[2] See NAR's guidance: www.nar.realtor/coronavirus-a-guide-for-realtors
[3] See https://youtu.be/0EExr7kIBHU

3. The hiring client (i.e. real estate agent) may meet the photographer at the property but must wear a face covering at all times and stay at least six feet away from the photographer at all times. It is recommended that a lockbox be left for the photographer instead to reduce the risk of exposure.

4. Once the photographer begins work, the hiring client, if meeting the photographer at the property, must not be inside the property and must remain out of the property until the photographer has left.

5. All lights must be turned on prior to the photographer's arrival (to avoid touching surfaces).

6. The house must be noticeably clean and sanitary. It is left to the discretion of the photographer that if there is any doubt in sanitation, the photographer may leave the property immediately.

7. Once the photographer begins working, no one may enter the property, not even the owner or hiring client, until the photographer has left the property.

8. The photographer is to wear a face covering while inside the property at all times.

I also suggest getting door-hangers that warn people to stay out of the property due to Covid-19.[4] Once you enter the property, hang these on all entrance doors and make sure all entrance doors are locked.

Given the growing culture of social distancing, face coverings, and safety in general, these simple protocols should never be questioned by your clients. If someone complains about this, I recommend dropping that job and moving on. Anyone who can't respect your health and safety is not a client worth keeping.

---

[4] See these hangers: https://amzn.to/3f2lXJw

Virtual Tour Basics

When I started shooting real estate I was stunned to see what some were calling "virtual tours", which were essentially just slideshows of still photos. That is NOT a virtual tour by today's standards, and it's not what's covered in this book. Instead, a *real* virtual tour is a user experience that allows the viewer to move around and through a property using a kind of virtual reality interface, like this:

http://virtual-tour-book.remotehomeshowings.com/example-2

A common way to do this today is by shooting 360° panoramas and hosting them on a 360/virtual-tour provider. That's what this book will cover, from start to finish.

Before digging into all of this, I'd like to take a few pages to cover the basics of 360° virtual tours, setting the foundation for the rest of the book.

360 vs. 3D

You may see or hear some refer to virtual tours as being 3D, but this is often an inaccurate, yet commonly accepted term for virtual tours. Pictures and videos in 3D format usually require special glasses to perceive all three dimensions with a noticeable change in depth of field throughout the view. Most virtual tours today though — including the ones in this book — are not *really* 3D; more accurately, they are 360. The nit-picky difference is that 360° virtual tours are made with *spherical* panoramas, which, although you can navigate in all spatial dimensions while viewing them, are actually displayed in two dimensions at any given time (not three). Sure, you can spin around in all directions, but your view at any given time is still in two dimensions. Being spherical is where the term 360 comes from, but since most people tend to relate to the term 3D more than 360, many people call these tours 3D. You can call them whatever you feel is appropriate for your market; however, since the more accurate term is 360, that's what I'll be using throughout the rest of the book.

360° Photography Overview

Unlike other genres of photography, 360° photography is not intended to be printed on paper. This style of photography is viewed on a screen — a computer, phone, tablet, VR goggles, etc. — since it's the interactive, virtual experience that this genre of photography offers. In many ways this is no different from other real estate photography you may be doing since listings are mostly viewed online through websites. So although creating 360° photos may be different than shooting standard real estate photos, many of its processes are similar (like post processing).

In recent years, 360° photography was seen by many as merely a kind of toy to post on social media, where one could spin around an image of you and your cat to look up, down, and all around — a gimmick of sorts. Although this style of art has been around since the 18th century — when painter Robert Baker created panoramic paintings and later in the 19th century when photographers shot panos and placed them in spinning, viewing carousels — recent marketing needs for a virtual experience have refined and brought to the forefront a new way of showing real estate (and other such things) using 360° photography.

The principle for creating 360° photography is to create what's known as a "spherical panorama". I'll keep it simple and often just refer to these as "360 panos", which are often called "scenes" once they are part of a virtual tour. Once you have such an image, you upload it to a 360 host that provides the virtual tour interface that allows viewers to move around this spherical pano. Being a fairly new form of media to many, some would perceive these spinning panos as videos, and some clients refer to them as such; however, calling them *video* is incorrect. A 360° video is indeed a video that was recorded with a 360 camera, but it's not the subject of this book. Here we'll discuss 360° photography hosted through a web provider, which is viewed and driven by the user's experience.

Capturing the 360 pano can be the trickier part, but with today's tech it can be fairly simple — just perhaps different than you're accustomed to. Up until a few years ago, 360 panos were shot using a DSLR, which you can still do today with high-end results, and which I'll also show later in the book. The more complicated DSLR process involves using a panoramic head on your tripod, mounted with your DSLR using a fisheye lens, taking four shots in a circle (each 90° apart), and then one shot up and one optional shot down, that get stitched together into the 360 pano using special software. This older, DSLR approach to 360 panos, while being the quality king of 360 has been supplanted in large part by quicker gear (portable 360 cameras) that sacrifice quality for speed, creating virtual tours faster, but with a tough time getting professional results. This book will cover both techniques: portable 360 cameras and using DSLRs. I use both as well — something else I'll explain further throughout the book.

The new, popular tech for capturing 360 panos are often called portable 360 cameras, which are small, usually thin cameras with a fisheye lens on either side, allowing you to capture an entire spherical, 360° panoramic photo in one shot. The time savings becomes obvious compared to the DSLR approach that requires usually 4-6 images to make a pano, and there are pluses and minuses to both approaches, each of which I'll cover in this book. Some of the pros and cons of each approach are:

Issue	DSLR	Portable 360 Camera
Image Quality	Extremely high, as high as your DSLR's sensor and lens allow.	Poor to fair. You are at the mercy at whatever the camera comes with, and many portable 360

		cameras struggle with quality.
Window Views (i.e. window pulls)	Excellent, provided you follow the same techniques used for other interior photography using such things as window pulls that get a clear view to the outside of a home when shooting in it (discussed in my interiors book and lighting guide).	Hit and miss, at best. Since you can't use flash you have to either cut-in windows, leave them blown out, or, as I'll show later in the book, feather them in to some degree using luminosity masking.
Shooting Effort	Somewhat involved in that multiple shots need to be taken.	Fast. Set up the camera, step out of the room, and fire away using a mobile app.
Editing Effort	Low. Besides a few added steps specific to 360° photography, editing is pretty much like you would for all of your other real estate photography workflows. However, there are times when software can struggle to create your 360 panos in something known as the stitching process, so with all fairness,	High. To get pro quality out of most portable 360 cameras you'll constantly fight noise in shadows, light bloom from windows, lens flairs, hit-and-miss color quality, and unacceptable chromatic aberrations. All of this can be adjusted to some degree in post processing, but the time you save

	there are rare occasions when a little more effort is required to make things right.	shooting with a portable 360° camera could be offset by the amount of editing required to produce pro results.
Workflow	Simple, and quick (most of the time). This is pretty much the same as all of your other real estate photography workflows.	Highly varied, and often frustrating. Each 360 camera manufacturer has their own stitching software, and not all play nicely with TIFF files to do high-end, pro quality editing. Some don't even load RAW files generated by their own cameras.
Battery Life	Great. Most DSLRs have batteries that can allow you to shoot multiple locations in a day, or even a week.	Poor to very poor. These smaller cameras tend to eat up battery power fast. For instance, shooting a standard size home takes about half a charge on the Ricoh Theta Z1, which, btw, doesn't have replaceable batteries (you have to charge the whole camera).
Damage risk	Low risk. If something happens to a lens, camera	High risk. Damage one thing on most portable 360°

	body, battery, etc. you just change the individual part.	cameras and you are basically left with a paperweight as the camera becomes entirely useless without sending it in for repair.

To see the difference in quality, I have an example tour online with the exact same pano shot with a DSLR and a Ricoh Theta Z1 (the best of the portable 360° cameras in this book), at this link:

virtual-tour-book.remotehomeshowings.com/dslr-vs-thetaz1-examples

There is a menu at the top left to switch between the two. The Theta Z1 example could be improved by using color layers and other advanced editing in Photoshop (something I'll cover later in the book), yet there is no simple way to get clear views outside, sharpness, and other things that are obvious in the DSLR example.

For these reasons I suggest trying both approaches. By having the ability to shoot high-end 360 with a DSLR and quick 360s with a portable camera, you can obtain a variety of work; never worry about having a backup; and best of all, you can offer mixed services with various pricing structures as well.

The Steps Involved

Creating a 360° virtual tour involves the following high-level steps, which I'll elaborate on throughout this book:

1. Photograph 360° panoramas. This is done with a 360° camera or a DSLR. The former is easiest while the latter is more time-consuming; however, as I'll show in this book, although DSLR

shooting takes more time, the results are hands-down, phenomenally better compared to using a portable 360° camera.

2. Stitch the panoramas. This is a process required no matter what camera you are using (portable 360 or DSLR) to create seamless 360 panos. Most 360° camera manufacturers provide their own stitching software, and there are third party companies that provide this as well (for instance, if using a DSLR you'd have to use third party software, like PTGui).

3. Edit. Like any other digital photography, you can edit these panos (most of the time) to correct colors, highlights, shadows, exposure, remove items, etc. Lightroom and Photoshop, in fact, can be used for much of this process.

4. Host the 360° panos. In order to view the 360 panos in a virtual experience you will need to host these panos somewhere. There are new 360 hosts popping up all the time, and I'll discuss some that I recommend.

5. Add link- and info-spots. These are arrows and icons that you add once the 360 panos are hosted to allow the viewer to navigate from room to room, scene to scene, or provide information about a feature.

Nadirs and Zeniths

Since a 360° pano can be navigated in all directions, a viewer can look straight up and straight down, which can complicate things a bit. The view straight up is known as the "zenith" and the view straight down is called the "nadir" (pronounced NAY-DUR in the US, and NAY-DEER in the UK). The zenith is really no big deal, except when shooting 360 panos with a DSLR, which requires you capture that in a separate shot. The more complicated issue is the nadir; specifically, what to do with what lies below your camera.

For most of my work I leave the nadir as-is; in other words, if someone wants to go to the bother of looking straight down, then say hello to my camera, stand, tripod, or a patch I might place there. However, if you are shooting for a high-end client, say a housing designer where capturing the floor is crucial, then there are ways to deal with getting a better looking nadir: either editing it out, or, if shooting with a DSLR, taking a separate shot for the nadir (slightly away from where the tripod is). Also, you can add a nadir patch, something I'll show in the "Editing Workflows" chapter. Some photographers will lock the horizontal view in their tours, which prevents users from looking straight up or straight down, but that's something I don't recommend.

You will though see throughout the book that while I always include the zenith, I often skip the nadir. This will make learning 360° photography easier. Then once you've reached your comfort level with creating virtual tours, you can refer to the sections in this book on nadir patching (in the "Editing Workflows" chapter), or try shooting nadirs as well.

Gear

This chapter covers gear for both ways of shooting 360 panos: with a portable 360° camera or using a DSLR. After discussing the gear for each, I'll touch on a hybrid approach to combine these two, and then briefly discuss a couple other gear options to think about.

Portable 360° Camera Gear

There are a slew of portable 360° cameras available today, many of which though are geared toward action sport video, not able to provide pro quality stills for taking 360 panos. While it would be nearly impossible to talk about each one, there are a few I've bought, tested, and used in the field. Along with a portable 360° camera is a stand to mount it on, which might seem trivial, but there are important things to consider, so after covering a few cameras real quick, I'll talk about options for mounting these portable cameras.

Ricoh Thetas

Ricoh has made a line of portable, "prosumer" 360° cameras that rival many others at their price point. The Theta Z1 is their recent camera that comes with one-inch sensors at 23MP.[5] This is a decent camera, but it's far from perfect. While being one of the best portable cameras for shooting 360 panos, it lacks the higher quality you would get from using a DSLR. Coming in at around $1,000 this is a bit pricey compared to its competitors, but there are other, lower quality Ricoh cameras like the Theta V, which runs about 1/3 the cost of the Z1. As with most things in life, you get what you pay for, and the V is inferior to the Z1. The

---

[5] See https://amzn.to/2BJgjhh

V is a less expensive option, but it's not on my recommend list for professional real estate photography.

It's important to also note that the Ricoh Theta Z1, although it shoots in RAW format, it — like other prosumer 360 cameras — has atrocious signal-to-noise ratio. This will put a lot of grain/noise in shadows, even when shooting at the Z1's incredibly low ISO 80. This can be improved without sacrificing too much quality by two methods I'll talk about later in the book: Exposure Blending using luminosity masks, and with Lightroom presets as well.

The Theta Z1 has an adjustable aperture, allowing you to shoot at f/5.6. Many other portable 360 cameras have fixed apertures around f/2, which doesn't provide good depth of field, often leaving distant objects soft. That though isn't a problem with the Z1. Take for instance the difference in depth of field, assuming a focal length of 7mm (for the fisheye lenses using a 35mm equivalent), and a subject distance/focal-point of two feet:

Subject/Focus Distance = 2'		
Aperture	**Near Limit**	**Far Limit**
f/2.0	1.5'	4'
f/5.6	1'	Infinity

To achieve infinity at f/2.0 on a 7mm focal length, the camera's locked focus would need to be 4' or greater, which is a stretch for many portable 360 cameras (3' at 5mm focal length). Many portable 360 camera manufacturers don't include focus range (or focal length) with their specs, so getting the facts on their focusing isn't readily available. But, I think you can see the difference that f/5.6 can provide. I can also say from my testing that the Ricoh Theta Z1 is sharper and better focused than the other two cameras I'll talk about in this book (the QooCam 8K and Insta360 One X). However, the Ricoh Theta Z1 still won't be as sharp as using a DSLR for shooting 360 panos, but it is the sharpest of the portable 360 cameras I've researched, bought, and tested.

Another thing to note about the Z1 is that it has no changeable power or storage (no changeable battery or SD cards, they're built-in). The Z1 eats a lot of power, and after one shoot I'm often left with 1/2 battery power, making it tough to shoot more than one virtual tour in a day. To overcome this, I bring along a portable power bank to charge my Z1 between shoots. I either charge the Z1 on my drive to the next shoot, or I charge it on-site, like in the last room I'll shoot where I hide my gear bags and cases (I tend to shoot virtual tours after everything else, photos, video, etc.). This is obviously annoying, and I hope that future releases of this or a similar camera from Ricoh will have changeable batteries, and storage.

QooCam 8K

Coming in at about $600, the QooCam 8K[6] is affordable, but not something I'd recommend over the Ricoh Theta Z1. Although the QooCam has decently sized sensors (1/1.7" compared to 1/2.3" on the Insta360 One X), those sensors are about half the size of the Z1, which has 1" sensors (QooCam's are about 0.6"). The QooCam 8K has a number of downsides for taking stills, but I think this can work as a backup camera to pull out in a pinch. Still, I couldn't imagine using this on a regular basis for pro work, but if you can't get hold of a Ricoh Theta Z1 or you need a backup, then the QooCam 8K is a potentially viable option.

A major problem (or perhaps annoyance) I found with this camera is that it runs hot. And I mean HOT! It even has a fan that runs full time to cool it off. After shooting with the QooCam 8K for 20 minutes it's so hot that I wouldn't feel comfortable putting it

---

[6] See https://amzn.to/2XIMbeC

back in its case/sleeve. And if you ever thought about using it for video, forget about audio since that fan would no doubt cause noise issues (unless you used a remote mic, far away).

The documentation for the QooCam is not that great, which makes using their touchscreen menus a difficult process to get used to. For instance, once you find the WiFi option (sliding the touch screen downward) you have to enable it every time you start the camera. And to transfer files to a PC, you have to go to the "Settings" menu (slide down also) and change the USB device to be "Mass Storage". I found that I had to do these steps every time I used the camera, making it highly annoying and time-consuming.

The QooCam 8K, like most portable 360° cameras, is a fixed-focus camera, and it only has one aperture: f/2. This leaves a shallow depth of field with many distant objects soft and not well focused. I also found this to have a fair amount of chromatic aberration, and the editing process was cumbersome (something I'll cover in the "Editing Workflows" chapter).

With all fairness to QooCam and other similar portable 360 cameras, their primary market appears to be action sports, and mostly consumers. In other words, these are more toys than tools, so the poor to fair results for the price-point are to be expected.

Insta360 One X and One R

The Insta360 One X (recently supplanted by the newer Insta360 One R Twin Edition) can work for 360° real estate virtual tours, and we've used the One X on some shoots; however, it takes a good amount of editing to get even semi-decent results. This is definitely more toy than tool, but it's the next best contender for a portable 360 camera — yet still last on my list. I've included it in this book since it (and the newer One R) can shoot RAW, and it can achieve somewhat OK results.

While writing this book, Insta360 is only providing the One X through Apple.[7] Just weeks ago I was able to purchase this through Amazon, but resellers there now are charging up to twice as much for the One X since Insta360 is now pushing their newer Insta360 One R. I haven't tested the One R camera, but at just $480 through Amazon (with free returns) I believe the One R (Twin Edition that includes 360) may be a viable, low risk option to try.

Stands

If you're shooting with a portable 360° camera then you'll want to use a sturdy light stand or something similar with the standard 1/4" thread mount — most 360° cameras have that mount. If you're shooting 360 panos with a DSLR, then stands are not needed but you will need a tripod (covered next). Since portable 360° cameras are often used by consumers, cheap selfie sticks that double as a stand are often offered in package deals, don't bother with those; they are way too flimsy and put your camera at high risk of a tip-over, especially outside from a light breeze, and they can move indoors from shot to shot if sitting on carpet, for instance. Instead, I recommend using a good light stand, like the Flashpoint Air Cushioned light stand[8] that I use for other photography (and recommend in some of my other books as well). This, like many other light stands, allows you to narrow its footprint quite a bit by pushing the center leg mount downward, like this:

---

[7] apple.com/shop/product/HMLM2ZM/A/insta360-one-x-camera-bundle
[8] adorama.com/fpls9.html

While the shot on the left is what you may be accustomed to when setting up a light stand (and pulling the center mount higher to collapse it) as the shot on the right shows, if you keep pushing that center mount down it will bring the legs inward, thus making for a smaller footprint.

This particular stand also has an easily removable 1/4" fitting that you can remove from the top of the stand, screw it into the bottom of your 360° camera, and then place the mounted camera back onto the light stand securely, as shown below:

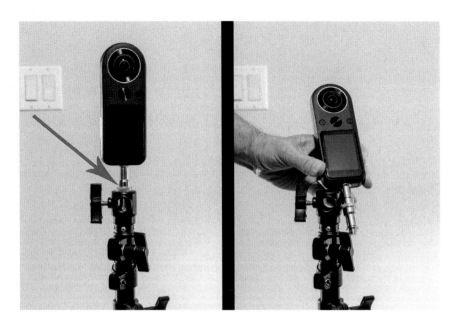

This lessens the risk of a drop or lens-touch while trying to spin your camera onto a stand. This allows you to keep the camera near a more comfortable area (near its case, table top, etc. versus 4' above the floor where it could fall to meet its doom). Simply remove the mount from the light stand, screw it into the base of your portable 360 camera, and then replace the mount (with camera attached) onto the light stand. I feel much safer using this then trying to spin one of these portable cameras onto the mount while not touching the lenses on either side of the camera.

Cases

Portable 360 cameras tend to come with cheap, neoprene sleeves, which don't fully protect the lenses on the camera. Instead, I recommend getting a hard-shell case, like this one for the Ricoh Theta Z1:

https://amzn.to/2XYVp56

...or perhaps this one for an Insta360 One X:

https://amzn.to/2AALlHq

Pelican makes small cases as well, like their 1120 model, which should be just big enough to fit many portable 360 cameras:

https://amzn.to/2BnbnhL

Remote Control

You can control most portable 360° cameras with practically any mobile device using WiFi, allowing you to change exposures and shoot from a distance, out of view. Most portable 360° cameras come with a free app you can use on your phone or tablet. These are crucial to not only remotely firing your camera so that you can hide out of sight, but also for changing exposure settings. Often you can go to the camera manufacturer's website and they will have a link to these apps, or you can search for them in your platform's store (i.e. Apple's App store).

While you can control the camera with your phone, I suggest using a small tablet instead. I've had to reboot 360° cameras when I got a call or text on my phone, sending the camera's controlling app into some kind of chaotic loop — this even happened using the preferred Ricoh Theta Z1, and I had to reboot the camera multiple times for it to finally recover. For this reason alone I'd recommend using a tablet that is not receiving any texts or emails, and you will also have a bigger screen to see how well you're setting exposures; the previews from a 360 camera are much wider than what you see from a DSLR so they're pretty small on a phone.

I like to use the iPad mini,[9] which runs about $400. You don't need the cellular option, just WiFi. It's small enough to tuck into any gear bag or case and hand-carry around, yet big enough to see the previews more clearly than on a phone.

---

[9] See https://amzn.to/30hViUZ

DSLR Gear

The ultimate option for shooting 360° panoramas is to use a DSLR. The results are, hands down, far better than using any portable 360° camera (at least the prosumer models). Using a DSLR you have all the flexibility you would shooting any other real estate photography, including the ability to use flash, which also allows you to do window pulls for tack-sharp views to the outside. Much of the gear needed for doing this you may already have, with the exception of a few items.

Below is a shot of my basic DSLR setup (minus the flash trigger, which is optional depending on the method you use). Each of the subsections below has links to items in this shot, along with other gear you may need.

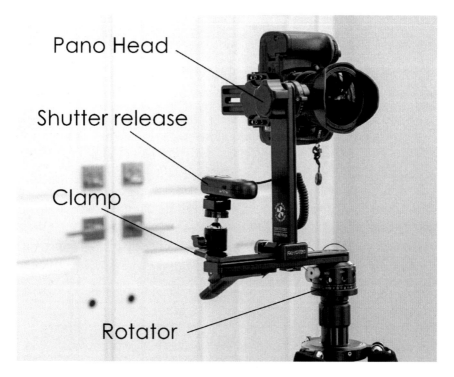

Camera Body

Almost any DSLR can be used to shoot a 360 pano. If you're already working as a real estate photographer then you've likely got this covered, so I won't spend much time here talking about what camera body is better than another. For 360° photography, almost any DSLR will be better than the portable 360° cameras, even if you don't use flash (I'll cover shooting with and without flash later in the book).

As you may know from my other books and videos, I prefer to shoot full-frame for everything, so I have multiple Nikon D610s and D750 bodies, which I can pop a lens on for shooting 360s (I'll talk about lenses next). I do recommend dedicating a camera body to a lens for shooting 360 panos as this will greatly reduce setup time — something I'll discuss in the "DSLR, Initial Setup" section in the "Photographing a 360" chapter. By having a single body with a permanent lens attached, you can quickly mount that setup onto your pano head and get to work. Since any DSLR is better than most (if not all) portable 360 cameras, your DSLR-lens pair shouldn't cost you an arm and a leg, and it'll likely be very comparable to the price of a good portable 360 camera like the Ricoh Theta Z1.

I prefer to buy refurbished camera bodies (not used; *refurbished*). Buying refurbished saves me a fair amount of money for a camera that comes with new internals (usually new sensor and shutter mechanism); for instance, you can pick up a refurbished D750 for about $1,000 at B&H Photo. And, Amazon has "Amazon Renewed" D610 bodies for about $700.[10] Bottom line: keep your 360 DSLR camera investment reasonably low as it, no matter what brand or format, will no doubt be better quality than most portable 360° cameras.

---

[10] See https://amzn.to/30gryYC

Fisheye Lens

Although you can use almost any lens to shoot a 360 pano with a DSLR, a fisheye lens is preferred. Vertical and barrel distortion — unacceptable items in *regular* real estate photography — aren't an issue when shooting 360 panos since those issues will be corrected in the post processing step known as "stitching" (where a wrap-around image is created with distortion correction). Fisheye lenses allow more of a scene to be captured, and in fact are implemented on most portable 360 cameras as well.

If you are using a full-frame camera then you'll want to use a fisheye lens with a focal length no greater than 12mm. If you are using a crop-sensor camera, then 8mm. I like using the Samyang F/2.8 12mm lens, which costs about $350 and comes in Nikon, Canon, and Sony E mounts.[11] For crop sensor cameras, you may consider the Rokinon 8mm F/3.5 lens, although I haven't tested that particular lens[12] (I shoot entirely full-frame for all of my work).

No matter what fisheye lens you end up using for shooting DSLR 360 panos, you really — or at least *almost* — can't go wrong. The combination of any DSLR with almost any fisheye lens will more than likely be higher quality than what you'd get from a portable 360° camera.

Pano Head

A must-have item for shooting 360 panos with a DSLR is a panorama head (or just "pano head" for short). This will allow you to adjust your camera's placement so that, as you rotate the camera on this head, you will avoid what's known as a "parallax error" (I'll show how to adjust your pano head for that in the "DSLR, Initial Setup" section in the "Photographing a 360" chapter).

---

[11] Samyang FF lens: https://amzn.to/3cJcTrD
[12] Rokinon crop sensor lens: https://amzn.to/3h6b0IM

I use the Nodal Ninja 6,[13] which is well built and very precise, with a camera mount that is built to keep your camera from tilting once mounted. Nodal Ninja makes other pano heads like the Nodal Ninja 3, made for mirrorless and smaller DSLRs.

Coming in at around $400 for a Nodal Ninja 6, I believe it's a worthwhile investment, but there are less expensive options, like the Neewer Gimbal Head,[14] which runs about $50 to $100, and also the Sunwayfoto head,[15] which runs about $250. Higher quality pano heads tend to provide more consistent results, making the stitching processes easier. In particular, the Nodal Ninja 6 and Sunwayfoto heads have a flange on the back of the camera mounting plate to ensure the camera doesn't drift downward. Cheap pano heads often don't have this, and their mechanisms overall may not be as sturdy, which is something you'll appreciate if you start shooting a lot of 360 panos with a DSLR.

Tripod

Tripods are mandatory for shooting 360 panos with a DSLR. Any good tripod will work fine, like the Feisol Tournament Tripod[16] that I recommend in my other books. This is a great carbon fiber tripod that runs about $420, making it a very worthwhile investment for not just 360° photography, but for all of your other real estate photography as well. I also recommend getting the center column for this tripod, which runs about $40, but that's optional.

I prefer to dedicate one of my tripods to my 360 DSLR setup. Since you will be rotating a pano head on the tripod, if you rotate the head counterclockwise then you could unintentionally start unscrewing the head from the tripod; conversely, if you tighten the pano head enough so that it doesn't unscrew from the

[13] NN6 at BH Photo: https://bhpho.to/3h0JeNT
[14] Neewer head: https://amzn.to/2LMqhjQ
[15] Sunwayfoto: head https://amzn.to/2U6BGPO
[16] Feisol tripod: https://amzn.to/2Wg22AE

tripod, then you could have a tough time removing the head, since rotating the head also rotates not just the base but the pano head's rotator as well. It's not so much a safety issue as it is an annoyance that could waste time while on-site, so I just keep my pano head mounted to one of my tripods at all times. This is just an observation from personal experience, not a hard-fast rule — all tripod heads, pano included, can be switched out at any time.

Lights/Flash

Flash is optional when shooting interior 360 panos with a DSLR, but it's something I recommend. Since most portable 360 cameras don't have flash-triggering capabilities, using a DSLR similarly without flash provides higher quality images than most portable 360 cameras. With that said though, I prefer to use flash for my interior 360 panos for two main reasons:

1. To get correct color. By adding just a puff of flash I can get good colors, and then do *global* flash-ambient blend with my ambient shot. I'll talk more about this in the "Photographing a 360" chapter in the section on DSLR footage.

2. To add window pulls, using the same darken-mode window technique I show in my interiors book.

This becomes a somewhat involved operation since, at a minimum, instead of having five shots (four around and one up) I might have 10 shots (ambient and flash shots for each), possibly up to 15 if I get crazy with window pulls. Each of the five positions shooting this DSLR footage needs to have the same exposure settings as well so that stitching is seamless. Nevertheless, I find the results worth the effort and my pricing structure compensates commensurately, so I do recommend flash photography for interior 360 panos shot with a DSLR. This though isn't the same as lighting a space for your interior photography, and in some regards, it's simpler.

Bear in mind that the goal of using a DSLR for 360 panos is to provide better results than a portable 360 camera, yet the fisheye lens will capture every detail including flash blooms. But by keeping it simple, you can get by with just a single pop of flash behind the camera, which means you really only need one flash unit. Using just one flash, I prefer to use the AD200Pro,[17] which is just small enough to put in my back pocket, fired using a Godox trigger in the camera's hot-shoe (I'll talk about triggers next). Any Godox trigger will do since you will want to adjust your flash power manually (more on why later in the book). The AD200Pro has enough power to give a pop of flash in almost any circumstance, and do window pulls too.

Another important point regarding flash for 360 panos is that your exposure settings should be such that you don't need to flash the entire space; just dominate the white balance (similar to regular interior photography, auto white balance is preferred when using flash for 360 pano footage). And of course darken-mode window pulls don't require much flash power under almost any circumstance. Once again, I'll cover this in more detail in the section on DSLR footage. The take-home point here is that, if you want to use flash for your 360 panos using a DSLR, keep it simple and just use one portable unit.

Flash Trigger

If you are using flash then you will need to have a flash trigger in your camera's hot-shoe. If you are using the AD200Pro that I recommended in the last section, then almost any Godox or Flashpoint trigger will work, like the Flashpoint R2 Pro trigger,[18] which is the same as the Godox Xpro trigger.[19] Or, you could also use the R2 SP single-pin transmitter,[20] since using flash when shooting 360 panos doesn't require any adjustments from the

---

[17] AD200Pro: https://amzn.to/2LQgkBS
[18] R2 Pro trigger: https://amzn.to/3craMs9
[19] Godox Xpro trigger: https://amzn.to/3eBEHzx
[20] R2 SP transmitter: https://amzn.to/3eDAUl9

trigger; using just one flash unit you can manually adjust the power on the flash itself, not the trigger.

No matter what trigger you decide to use, be aware that some smart triggers can cause issues with auto white balance, which I'll cover next.

White Balance Issues with Triggers

As you may recall from my lighting guide or in some of my YouTube videos,[21] smart triggers can affect auto white balance, even when used in manual, non-TTL mode. A smart trigger (like the Flashpoint R2 Pro) sitting in your camera's hot-shoe can be detected incorrectly by your camera since many trigger manufacturers falsely identify their smart triggers, no matter what mode the trigger is in. The camera then uses this false information in its auto white balance (AWB) calculations, which throws things off. Ideally, trigger manufacturers should disable device identification when their triggers/transmitters are in manual, non-TTL mode — but not all do. For instance, when using the Nikon version of the R2 Pro transmitter, my Nikon cameras detect the trigger as an SB-900 speedlight (visible in the EXIF data). This false information is used by the camera to adjust its AWB calculations, resulting in warmer photos, off by as much as 500-800 Kelvin. But there are ways to fix this.

The problem comes from smart transmitters using more than just the center pin in the camera's hot-shoe. Dumb triggers usually have only a center pin, which is the contact that tells whatever is in the hot-shoe to fire. The other pins are for camera intelligence, which we don't need since everything we shoot for 360 panos is manually controlled. To avoid this issue, there are a few things you could do:

1. Use a hot-shoe adapter that uses only the center pin in the hot shoe (like this: https://amzn.to/36NQisJ).

---

[21] Watch video at https://youtu.be/RCQO24hcjMo

2. If you're using Godox or Flashpoint lights, then you could use the R2 SP single-pin transmitter, which only has a single pin.

3. Use a smart trigger made for a different camera OEM; for instance, if you have a Nikon camera then use a smart trigger for a Canon camera. The different OEMs shouldn't be able to detect the device the smart transmitter is advertising, so the camera should throw away this information when doing its AWB calculations. This isn't a guaranteed method, but one that should work on most cameras.

4. Tape over the contacts (with non-conductive, electrical tape) on a regular hot-shoe adapter. You could tape over the contacts on your camera's hot shoe, but I'd recommend doing that to a $15 adapter, not a $1500 camera.

5. Trigger-stack a dumb trigger between the camera's hot-shoe and the smart transmitter. Many dumb triggers only have a center pin, so having a dumb trigger in your camera's hot shoe with the smart trigger mounted into the dumb trigger's hot-shoe eliminates contact with all pins except the center pin. Most dumb triggers need to be switched to TX (transmit) mode to work as a pass-through device from your camera's hot-shoe to the smart trigger.

Remote Control

Controlling your DSLR can use the same gear and method you use for regular interior photography. If you're using a Camranger or other remote device then you're good to go. If you use the technique I show in my other books with using shutter-release triggers and setting your camera's exposure manually using the camera's thumbwheels, then this too is acceptable (it's what I do) but make sure you don't have your pano head mounted on top of another head, which could be tempting to help level it (like mounting your pano head on a geared head). Those stacked heads will create more wobble as you touch your camera.

Also, take care that whatever is plugged into your camera for remote control is completely out of sight, since a fisheye lens will pick up a lot more than you may be accustomed to. In fact, you will want to step slightly back, away from the camera for your rotational shots, and crouch down for the zenith shot. For the setup I showed in the image at the beginning of this DSLR gear section, the shutter release and clamping mechanism comprises the following parts:

- Clamp with ballhead: https://amzn.to/3eXWph1

- Cold shoe adapter: https://amzn.to/3fbY0Qr

- Yongnuo shutter release with cable (for Nikon, there are other pairs for Canon, etc.): https://amzn.to/2A1HIKD

The Hybrid Approach

Not all of the 360° panos you shoot for a property need to be done with a single camera. For instance, you can have a package for luxury real estate that includes high-quality DSLR panos for main living areas, and lower-quality panos from portable cameras for other, less important rooms (like spare bedrooms, non-master bathrooms, laundry, etc.). So don't limit yourself to shooting one way or another, as you can charge for various packages that will compensate you for the efforts either way. I'll cover more on that in the "Pricing" chapter near the end of this book.

Pro 360 Cameras

If you want to enter the high-end world of 360 photography but you don't want to use a DSLR, then there are pro-level 360 cameras you might consider. Full disclosure: I don't own any of these, and I've only considered possibly getting one or two if we got long term corporate contracts that include either virtual reality video or tight spaces (like car interiors). Although this section is the only and last time I'll talk about them in this book, I'd be remiss if I didn't at least mention them and provide some links so that you can check them out for yourself.

Insta360, the same company that makes the inexpensive One X and One R, has the Insta360 Pro 2, which runs about $5,000. Their Insta360 Pro is a bit less expensive at $3,500, and their mega camera, the Insta360 Titan, runs a whomping $15,000. These kinds of cameras are not really in the realm of real estate photography, and are likely overkill for most real estate virtual tours. But, if the path of 360 takes you down a road of other opportunities, then this would be a good place to start your research for gear to get you the proper bang for your buck.

Hosting Services

Once you create 360 panos, you will need someplace to host them in a virtual tour. With 360-photography becoming more popular over the past few years, new hosts are coming into this market often, and it would take volumes to talk about them all. There are also free alternatives to consider. To keep things simple, in this chapter I'll briefly talk about a few hosting options to consider, and then later in the book I'll cover the steps to deliver your tours through a service in the "Hosting" chapter.

In short, my two recommendations for hosting 360 virtual tours for real estate are:

1. Cloudpano

2. Self-hosting using Marzipano.

I'll talk about those two options first, and then a few other options you may want to look at. Hosting services are fairly simple to use and don't need much explanation, so I'll keep this chapter brief, talking about their benefits and/or shortcomings to help you decide what hosting services may work well for your real estate photography business.

CloudPano

Cloudpano (cloudpano.com) is my turnkey virtual tour hosting service of choice as they are well priced, reliable, easy to use, and offer enough features to make my virtual tours. Cloudpano costs $33/month (if paid annually), and it's free to try. Some of their features include:

- Unlimited tours.

- Unlimited scenes (each 360 pano) in tours.

- The ability to clone a tour so that you can quickly make branded and unbranded tours.

- The ability to include a floor plan. You have to create the floor plan using something other than Cloudpano (like Magicplan, Cubicasa, RoomScan Pro, or similar floor plan app) and upload a JPG. It's not as feature-rich as Matterport, Cupix or EyeSpy360 (which I'll cover later in this chapter), but it is an option.

- A tie-in to Google Analytics for tracking.

- The ability to self-host your tours.

- Password-protect tours.

There's no risk or cost to try Cloudpano, and since this is my first recommendation, I would suggest visiting their website (cloudpano.com) and try it for yourself.

Marzipano (self-hosting)

Before talking about other virtual tour hosting services, I want to first discuss my second recommendation: the free DIY approach using Marzipano (marzipano.net). This is a very flexible tool for hosting 360 virtual tours, but it does take some tech knowledge to host — not to use, just to host. While there are companies that provide software development kits geared toward software developers wanting to create their own virtual tour services, Marzipano is one that I find not only useful, but super simple to use. All you need to do is launch their online Marzipano Tool (marzipano.net/tool) to create your virtual tour, similar to what you'd do with other hosting services (like Cloudpano). Then you export the tour, which generates all the files you need to host the tour yourself.

While Cloudpano also allows you to self-host your tours, Marzipano is free. Either way, self-hosting requires some level of web development experience to deploy your tours. For instance, you need know how to use FTP to transfer your files to your web host. If you're not familiar with things like FTP, then this likely won't be the way to go. But if you are, then I suggest giving Marzipano a try.

BTW: Marzipano expects 360 panos with a 2:1 ratio. While PTGui and other stitching programs may make your panos larger and many hosts like Cloudpano are OK with that, Marzipano isn't. I cover the fix in the "Hosting" chapter when discussing uploading to Marzipano.

Side note: example tours in this book were created using Marzipano, hosted on one of my websites.

Tourweaver (self-hosting)

While the rest of this chapter will discuss 360 hosts, if you are considering self-hosting and want to look at something other than Marzipano or Cloudpano, then Tourweaver[22] by Easypano may be an option.

Easypano is the company that makes Panoweaver, which is an alternative to PTGui for stitching 360 panos (something I'll cover later in the "Software" chapter in the section "Stitchers for DSLRs"). While more feature-rich than Marzipano, Tourweaver comes at a cost: about $300 for the Standard Edition, and about $900 for the Professional Edition. While this is virtual tour *software*, not *hosting*, it is an option for preparing your tours for self-hosting. If you are going down the self-hosting road, then I'll leave it to you to try this out for yourself as it is a more complicated option than turnkey hosting services like Cloudpano and others listed in this chapter. But, before going all-in on Marzipano — if that's the route you choose — then I would suggest that you give Tourweaver a look as well.

---

[22] Tourweaver: www.easypano.com/virtual-tour-software.html

Kuula

Kuula (kuula.co *note this is not a .com address, it's .co*) is a possible 360 virtual tour host to consider, but not at the top of my recommend list. While Kuula's pricing is similar to Cloudpano for the same or similar features (and less for a scaled-down version), Kuula doesn't provide a clearly defined way to contact them: no phone number on their website, and you have to dig into the footer of their web pages to get their contact email address. There is also no information on Kuula's website about their team or company either. These are things I'd expect from a pro company that I'd rely on for longevity, security, and consistency, so I don't feel comfortable using Kuula for my business.

Although it's not on my recommend list, the tours Kuula provides for their pricing makes them an attractive possibility — perhaps not today, but maybe over time once/if they grow. Kuula does have a free option, so with no risk you can give them a spin.

Cupix

Cupix (cupix.com) provides the ability to create virtual tours with a 3D effect similar to Matterport (covered next), where navigation has a 3D effect and they have true 3D floor plans as well. Cupix also allows you to upload your 360 panos yourself, so you can edit them prior to posting; however, editing may not be recommended for this kind of platform. Unlike 360 tours that show one scene at a time, Cupix shows the entirety of what you shot; in fact, instead of shooting just a room, you take shots every few feet or yards, providing Cupix with a scan of the area that their software will stitch together. This makes Cupix unique compared to most virtual tour hosts, but not necessarily something that I'd want for my photography business — at least not now. Being too unique and a recent start-up company (founded in 2015) with a technology I couldn't easily port to another provider has some risk, but price is where things get more complicated and difficult to justify.

Cupix's pricing structure[23] is quite complex as they base it on how much storage you will need, and what features you want as well. It's so complicated in fact, that they provide a calculator on their pricing page to help you try to figure out what package you may need. Using their calculator revealed that if I used a Ricoh Theta camera on a 2,000 square foot house that I'd need anywhere from 27-160 MB of storage. Thus, at the upper end on for an average sized house this would mean that I could host about 6 virtual tours per gigabyte of storage, so using their price-competitive "Small" package of 3 GB ($24/month), I could only host 18 virtual tours. In other words, if I hosted one virtual tour a day, then I'd run out of storage in less than a month. To get ten times that much to last a year, let's say, then I'd have to pay for their "Large" package at $190/mo, or $2,280 per year. This kind of pricing structure assumes that you would retire/delete tours at some time, which is something I would not want to affect/drive my service provider budget.

Cupix provides something quite unique, and you can sign up for a free account, which gives you 250 MB of storage so you could host a tour or two to try them out. Cupix doesn't make much business sense for my real estate photography work, but that shouldn't stop you from exploring them as an option.

Matterport

It's worth mentioning one of the original 360 cameras and hosts, Matterport (matterport.com), although they are not on my recommend list. While Matterport used to require the use of their high-end Pro2 Camera (about $3,400) to use their services, they are now offering the option to use just their hosting services. This broadens their market to those wanting to pay less for gear using either the Ricoh Theta Z1, Insta360 One X, and a few other

---

[23] Cupix pricing: https://www.cupix.com/pricing.html

portable 360 cameras, competing now with companies like Cupix. This new software-only option makes Matterport attractive, but not without concern.

When a hardware business shifts to being a software service it's often a bad sign, which recent events agree. In 2019 Matterport raised yet another round of funding ($48 million)[24] and replaced their CEO; and when the Covid-19 crisis got underway — a time when 360 virtual tours became more popular — Matterport laid off 1/3 of its workforce in April 2020.[25] Meanwhile, sales of 360 cameras went through the roof — mostly out of stock in April and May 2020 — and more photographers started offering 360 virtual tours. So in the biggest boon for virtual tours, Matterport seems to be struggling.

For a company that's been around for nearly ten years, these things raise yellow flags on the field, especially since lower cost competitors (some free, in fact) are becoming more popular, making Matterport now one of many 360 hosts in this growing market. In any case, with so many new 360 cameras, 360 hosting services, and even floor-plan providers (a topic perhaps for another book?) popping up all the time, Matterport is not something I recommend. Besides the questionability of its longevity, there are two main reasons why Matterport isn't part of my services (or recommendations):

1. Matterport costs more than many other 360 hosts. For instance, you can pay $33/month to Cloudpano for unlimited tours, unlimited scenes in tours, and the ability to include floor plans (from another provider). Matterport charges more than twice as much at $69/month for something somewhat similar, limited to 25 active spaces, plus $14.99 for each floor plan.

2. Editing Matterport footage is not viable. Matterport's expensive camera is good quality, but to edit anything

---

[24] Matterport funding: https://techcrunch.com/2019/03/05/matterport-2
[25] Matterport layoffs: bizjournals.com/sanjose/news/2020/04/15/opendoor-carta-matterport-cut-hundreds-of-jobs-as.html

before uploading it to Matterport for hosting is hackable, at best — there's no clearly defined way suggested by Matterport to edit, let alone use flash or anything else you can do that I'll talk about in this book.

I realize there are those who find Matterport a viable tool for their business, but if you are just now getting into 360 photography then I'd suggest not using Matterport, at least initially; instead, once you come up to speed with the methods I show in this book, then perhaps revisit Matterport's services and determine if they can offer you something better for your business.

EyeSpy360

EyeSpy360 (eyespy360.com) is a fairly new contender in the virtual tour hosting space, founded in 2016. Their product looks very similar to Cupix and Matterport with a 3D floor plan for navigation, and they allow you to use any 360 camera, even a DSLR. Pricing may seem attractive at first at $15 per virtual tour of up to 15 photos plus $1 for every photo after that, plus a subscription fee of about $20/month. But this, like Cupix, can add up; for instance, if I did 20 virtual tours a month, then I'd pay $320/month, or a little over $3,800 per year. That's more than 12 times what you would pay for Cloudpano. The added features provided by EyeSpy360 don't justify this cost for my business, but if you are looking at Cupix- and Matterport-like features, then EyeSpy360 is one to consider as well.

Ricoh Tours

If you own a Ricoh 360 camera and you're not adept at photography workflows like editing, then Ricoh Tours (ricohtours.com) may be something to look at. But at $45/month with limited features, this is not on my recommend list. Still, if you have a Ricoh and you need a quick and simple approach to hosting your virtual tours, then this may be an option. But if that *is* the case, then much of this book wouldn't be useful for you since Ricoh Tours is an all-in-one mobile app that assumes you will only take single shots of a scene and let their app upload the images for you — no editing in-between. I see Ricoh Tours geared more toward agents/realtors that don't hire photographers and want to do tours themselves. But, if you:

1. Have a Ricoh camera and,

2. You need to get tours online immediately and,

3. You are not up to speed yet on shooting and hosting pro virtual tours...

...then Ricoh Tours may be a stepping-stone to consider. I wouldn't consider this a permanent solution for your real estate photography business; just a temporary hold-over if all else fails.

Photographing a 360

There are two ways to photograph a 360° panorama that I'll cover in this chapter and throughout the rest of the book:

1. With a portable 360 camera. These are small cameras that have a fisheye lens on either side, capturing a single 360° image with one shot.

2. With a DSLR. This is a more involved process where you use any DSLR, preferably with a fisheye lens, to capture four images in rotation, one shot up, and optionally one shot down. You can optionally incorporate flash for high-end results, but it isn't mandatory (both flash and no-flash methods will be covered in this chapter and throughout the book).

Later in the book I'll step through the editing workflows, software, hosting, and more. For now, this chapter will discuss capturing the footage to be used.

Between these two options for photographing a 360 pano, it might seem at first glance that option #1 (portable 360 camera) would be the best way to go as it would appear to be the quickest and most advantageous approach. But that's not always the case if you want to get professional results. Back in the "360° Photography Overview" section in the "Virtual Tour Basics" chapter, you may recall from the comparison table that quality is higher and editing time often less when shooting a 360 pano with a DSLR to get pro results. To see the difference in quality, I have an example tour online with the exact same scene shot with a DSLR and a Ricoh Theta Z1 at this link:

virtual-tour-book.remotehomeshowings.com/dslr-vs-thetaz1-examples

There is a menu at the top left to switch between the two so you can go back and forth to compare these two methods. The editing time was about equal on these two examples, but to take the Theta Z1 example to the next level to get it even close to pro work, it would have required much more editing time with color layers, adjustment layers, and a lot of other edits in Photoshop (something I'll cover later in the "Photoshop Edits" section of the "Editing Workflows" chapter). DSLR clearly wins out on quality and edit time for pro results, yet DSLR panos are more complicated to shoot and can be difficult in tight spaces. Because of this, there is no single solution to 360° photography for professional real estate; instead, a combination of using a portable 360° camera *and* DSLR can provide you with a variety of options and packages that you can offer to various clients.

So if your initial thought is to only browse the first section of this chapter (on portable cameras), I'd encourage you to also look at the DSLR section here as well. First though, no matter what camera you are using, we need to give some thought as to how we'll compose these shots, which is different from standard real estate photography.

Compositions

No matter what method you use to photograph your 360 panos (portable camera or DSLR) certain composition rules apply, which are unique to 360° photography. For instance, since we're shooting spherical images of an entire space, you may think of just placing the camera in the center of the room and snapping a single shot. This though could limit the view of your images. To optimally view 360 panos for real estate, there are five primary composition rules to consider:

1. Camera Height

2. Initial View Optimization

3. Room Navigations

4. Room Perspectives

5. Room Transitions

These basic rules of 360-photography composition can make a big difference in how your images will be displayed, and thus the perception of the property in your virtual tours.

Camera Height

There is a balance between displaying your images initially with correct verticals while being able to capture features that rely on camera height, like countertops, sinks, etc. Most of the time you can raise your camera to the height you normally would when shooting regular interior photography, often just above counter height, or about 4'. But there are exceptions.

If you are in a very large space with very high ceilings, then you may want to consider placing the camera at or just below eye level. This will help to give a better perspective with less distortion than a lower camera height.

If you are in a tight space, no matter what camera height you choose, you can start your initial view (covered next) with a tilt downward, like this:

While this tilt-down view would make me cringe for regular interior photography, in the world of 360 tours, users will move the scene up, down, and all around, so this initial view doesn't bother me, and instead shows more of the features at first glance. Also, some 360 hosts, as they auto-rotate the pano, will correct those verticals, like in this example using Marzipano:

virtual-tour-book.remotehomeshowings.com/tilt-down

No matter what camera height you use, it's acceptable to start your initial view tilted down; however, I recommend doing this only for tight spaces as larger rooms will look like a carnival funhouse with that kind of initial view.

If you are using a DSLR, then camera height can be important for capturing the zenith shot (the shot looking straight up). Since stitching software relies on common points across all of the images (zenith included), if you have your camera so high that you capture a featureless ceiling, then stitching can be problematic. So if you are using a DSLR and ceilings are low, then position camera height moderately and try to compose so that features are included in the zenith, like doorways, window frames, etc.

Initial View Optimization

Although a viewer can spin a 360 image around with their mouse (or finger on a phone), their *initial* view will be greatly limited if you place the camera in the center of the room, as shown in the diagram below:

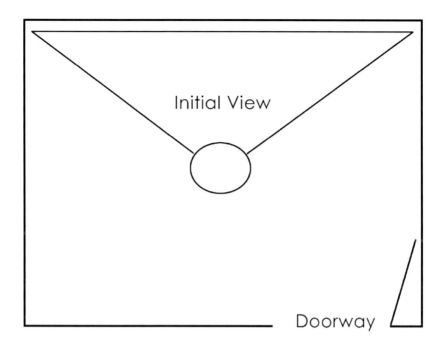

Although the camera is in the center of the room and capturing the entire room, when a person views this 360 pano they will only see a limited view at any given time. Thus, a room-centered composition means they will only see what lies from the camera's center — they can't see the entire room, or the most impactful portions of it without additional navigation (spinning around). To give your panos more punch, it's often best for real estate virtual tours to have the initial view contain more of a room, as shown in this next diagram:

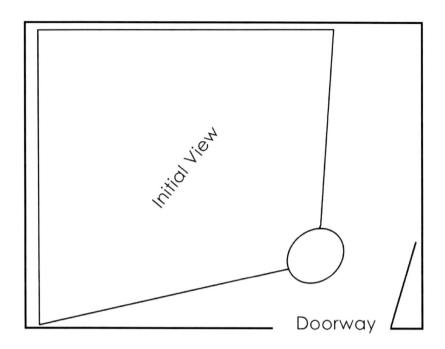

By placing the camera just inside of a room, you can set the initial view to show a much larger space. The downside is that when a user spins the 360 pano around to the opposite side they see a close view of a wall, or like in this case the door. This though is acceptable since this provides the first rule in real estate: space sells. We don't want to exaggerate the space to make it look bigger than it is, but if we placed the camera in the center of the room then we'd make the room look smaller than it is. Thus, there is a happy medium between the two extremes. I find that for small to medium sized rooms, placing the camera a couple feet inside the entry to a room works well, especially if the view can capture elements around the room like closet doors, doors to other rooms, hallways, etc. that will be in the virtual tour.

But like all rules, there are exceptions. If you're working in a big space, then placing the camera a couple feet from one corner will make it hard to navigate the entire space. Take this example:

virtual-tour-book.remotehomeshowings.com/example-dslr-family-dining

…where the space is so large that I placed the camera in the center of the scene. However, the camera is still on the edge of each room (between the living room and dining room).

Using this composition can also mean you may want to shoot more than one pano for a room, which is where the next composition, "Room Perspectives" comes into play.

Lens Direction

Whether you use a portable 360° camera or DSLR, initial view optimization is somewhat affected by the direction of your camera's lens(es). Unlike regular real estate photography, framing a 360 shot for composition is less critical since a 360 pano will include the entire scene. However, there are things to be aware of when deciding where to point your camera:

1. Lenses tend to be sharpest in the center and softest in the corners. This goes for all cameras (portable 360 and DSLR). Thus, it's often best to frame your pano so that the camera is pointing directly at your initial view. This is typically the most feature-rich area of the 360 pano. If you are using a portable 360° camera, then point one lens toward the center of that view. If you are using a DSLR, then this may be a good starting point for your first rotational shot; however, when using flash to include window pulls there are other things to consider.

2. If you are using a DSLR with flash, then you need to consider your effort for window pulls so that you have as few overlapping windows as possible. I'll touch on this again in the "Window Pulls" section of the "Using Flash" chapter.

3. You don't want a potential stitching error in the center of your initial view. Stitching errors can happen with any 360 camera (portable or DSLR), where a vertical line may appear over the entire height of the pano or a portion of it. This is most common at the highest and lowest points where fisheye distortion is greatest. If you point your camera directly at the most feature-rich area (your initial view), then any stitching

errors/lines will be outside of this important area. Stitching errors outside of the initial view are more forgiving and sometimes left as-is if it's: (a) Outside of the initial view and (b) Mostly in the upper- and/or lower-most areas of the frame.

Room Perspectives

Since you won't likely want to place your camera in the center of a room, it's often good do show large rooms from multiple points. Take this next example for instance, which btw, you can see this entire tour in action at this link:

virtual-tour-book.remotehomeshowings.com/example-2

In this screenshot from that tour, two of the arrows take the viewer to other corners of the room. Not only does this help the viewer see everything, but it also overcomes any issues with furniture or other obstacles that can block a particular view. Bedrooms don't usually need this, but if you are shooting a large living room or open-concept area, then you can shoot from various points to show how the room is laid out.

BTW: if you spun this pano around, you'd see the kitchen view, like so:

This though was not the initial view. This was just what you would see as you spin around. The barstools are very close to the camera, but with that view called "Living Room from Kitchen" and the initial view being the living room, one would expect to see this kind of proximity once you spun the pano around. The view of the barstools is more distant in other panos shot from other corners of this room.

One other thing to note here is that this particular example tour used the hybrid approach I mentioned earlier (using a DSLR with flash for the "money shots", and a portable 360 for everything else). For instance, take a look at the tour again at:

virtual-tour-book.remotehomeshowings.com/example-2

...and see if you can tell which two panos in this tour were *not* taken with a DSLR. Don't skip ahead yet...take a look first.

OK, ready for the answer? They are "Foyer", and "Living Room from Patio". Foyer was pretty much a no-brainer to shoot with just a portable 360° camera as it's an area that viewers won't spend much time browsing (it's just a transition space). The

"Living Room from Patio" though would have had better quality shooting with a DSLR, but since the initially view wasn't to the outside, I just used a portable 360 camera for that one too; granted though, it took a heck of a lot of editing to get that one to have views that looked halfway decent, and a DSLR would have been much better and with less editing time as well.

Room Navigations

Viewers need to know where to go as they browse a virtual tour, so it's important that, either with separate panos or somewhere in your panos, you include the following items:

1. Hallways: This allows you to navigate to various rooms. If a hall is L-shaped, you may try to get a shot at the corner of the hall, or feel free to take multiple hall shots, with navigation to each one. The key is to make sure that when you put your tour together you are able to place navigation arrows to rooms/scenes to and from other panos.

2. Views of the stairs: This is important for each floor so that viewers can navigate up and down the stairs. You don't need a separate pano for the stairs, but make sure that somewhere in some pano stairs are included on each floor.

3. Foyers: Similar to hallways, a foyer is a temporary navigation scene that viewers can use to jump from room to room (scene to scene).

Room Transitions

A room transition composition is when you have two adjoining rooms, like a bedroom with a bathroom, and taking a single shot can be quite effective between the two. Take this next, unedited shot for example, taken with a Theta Z1, which shows the views from both lenses:

The camera was positioned in the doorway between theses rooms so that one lens pointed into the bedroom while the other faced the attached bathroom. I often label these panos as "Bed-bath 1" (or whatever the bedroom number may be). The initial view is then set to the bedroom. This has some advantages, including:

1. If using a portable 360 camera, you can edit the white balance of each lens separately in post, which is easier than with an area that overlaps onto both lenses (something I'll cover in the "Selective White Balance" section of the "Editing Workflows" chapter).

2. You only need to shoot one pano, versus a separate pano for each room.

Because of the tight space, these are sometimes harder with a DSLR. But since smaller bedrooms like this aren't "money" shots, a portable 360 camera is usually the way to go.

I hosted 360 panos of room transition examples at this link:

virtual-tour-book.remotehomeshowings.com/room-transition-examples

All were shot with a Ricoh Theta Z1. These were mostly low impact scenes that likely wouldn't be browsed at length, so I skipped the DSLR for these.

Room transitions though can be shot with a DSLR as this composition works well in large rooms that benefit from higher end panos. Take for instance the example at this link:

virtual-tour-book.remotehomeshowings.com/room-transitions-dslr

...where the DSLR was positioned between the dining room and living room, allowing the user to clearly navigate both spaces from that particular perspective. While a portable 360 camera could be used as well, the results were better using a DSLR, and this particular shot was one of the "money shots" for the hybrid package I talked about earlier. The take-home point though is that you can use room transition compositions with any camera, but it is more often used with portable 360 cameras.

Now that we've covered *what* to shoot, it's time to talk about *how* to shoot. The next two sections of this chapter will cover shooting 360 panos using portable 360° cameras and DSLRs.

Portable 360 Cameras

The easiest way to shoot a 360 pano is with a portable camera. You just place it somewhere, step out of sight, and using a remote app (on your phone or a tablet), you take a shot. Although being easy to setup and shoot, the quality will be much lower compared to using a DSLR, especially if you shoot just a single image with your 360 camera. To improve the quality when using a portable 360 camera you should shoot multiple exposures that will later be blended — something I'll cover in the "Portable Camera Workflows" section of the "Editing Workflows" chapter. Still, the process for shooting is fairly straightforward; but you need to know what exposures to take, and how many.

Exposure Settings (Exteriors)

Shooting exteriors with a portable 360 camera is easiest outside. Typically you just need to take a single exposure, like so:

1. Set your portable 360 camera's mode to photo.

2. Set the shooting mode to Manual.

3. Set white balance to Auto. You can try setting Kelvin to 5,000 if your camera allows that, but Auto works well on most portable 360 cameras outdoors, and you will want to change white balance to Auto anyways once you step back inside to shoot interiors.

4. Set ISO to its lowest value. Many portable cameras go down to ISO 100, or lower.

5. Set the smallest aperture, if your camera allows it (smallest aperture is the highest f number). The Theta Z1, for instance, allows you to change aperture to f/5.6. Insta 360 One X and QooCam though are fixed aperture (around f/2), so you can't change their aperture.

6. Set the shutter speed. Depending on your camera's aperture, these are the settings I suggest trying for ISO 100:

ISO 100	
Aperture	**Shutter Speed**
f/5.6	1/400
f/2.8	1/1600
f/2.0	1/3200

These are starting points as each portable 360 camera tends to process exposures differently. Experiment with your camera to see what exterior exposures work well.

In any case, exterior exposure settings are single and easy. Interior exposures are more involved.

Exposure Settings (Interiors)

To get enough footage to create a decent quality interior pano from a portable 360 camera you may need to take anywhere from 3-10 exposures to blend later (once again, that'll be covered in the "Portable Camera Workflows" section of the "Editing Workflows" chapter). First and foremost is to use the best ISO and aperture your camera provides, then change only the shutter speed between shots. While this may sound straightforward, not all portable 360 cameras make it easy. Here are the steps:

1. Set your portable 360 camera's mode to photo.

2. Set the shooting mode to Manual.

3. Set white balance to Auto. This will often need to be adjusted in post, which I'll cover later in the book.

4. Set ISO to its lowest value. Many portable cameras go down to ISO 100, or lower.

5. Set the smallest aperture, if your camera allows it (smallest aperture is the highest f number). The Theta Z1, for instance, allows you to change aperture to f/5.6. Insta 360 One X and QooCam though are fixed aperture (around f/2), so you can't change their aperture.

6. Using the preview screen on your camera's app (on your phone or tablet), lower the shutter speed until you have a slightly overexposed image. This initial exposure is exposing for the shadows. Since most portable 360 cameras have atrocious noise in the shadows, the blending process we'll do later will reduce noise by taking this initial expose-for-the-shadows shot. For interiors this is often around 1/2 second at ISO 100, but sometimes I've had to go as low as 1.5 seconds.

a. Insta360 CAVEAT: This step is not easily done with the Insta360 One X since they only display the preview properly down to 1/30 second (another reason I don't recommend using a One X, and I got tired of arguing with their customer support about it). There is no good way to accurately take manual interior exposures with the Insta360 One X short of reviewing each shot taken, which is way too time-consuming. An alternative (which I hate, but here ya go) is to use ISO priority with ISO 100, then take a shot at 0 EV, one at +1EV, and another at -1EV. You could go further and expand that with other shots at higher EVs (i.e. +/- 2EV). The rest of these steps assume you are not using an Insta 360 One X.

7. After taking this initial, expose-for-the-shadows shot, take another shot at 2/3 stop higher (two increments on most shutter speed scales). You could go a full stop, but I find that 2/3 stop works best when working with exposure blending (the blending process I'll cover in the "Portable Camera Workflows" section later in the book).

8. Continue to take shots 2/3 stop higher until you have reached a point where highlights are mostly gone, or if a window view is required, that it looks clear outside.

At this point you should have a collection of footage similar to these 6 shots:

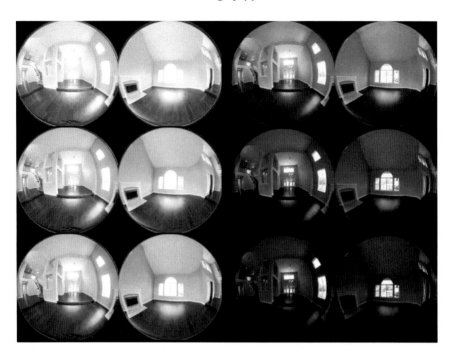

Notice how the first image in the top left looks overexposed, yet the shadows are well exposed. Then progressively the exposure was changed until we achieved a decent enough window view (not clear, just something besides being completely blown out.

We'll work with footage later in the "Portable Camera Workflows" section. The editing process can be harder than these steps to capture the footage, yet the opposite is the case if we go the DSLR route. That's covered next, and it may seem daunting at first, but I encourage you to slowly step though this next section as it can be a game changer for your virtual tour work.

DSLRs

The more involved method of shooting 360 panos for a virtual tour is using a DSLR, but don't let that deter you. The added effort results in a much higher quality product, and often with less editing than using a portable 360° camera — at least to get pro results. Whereas the portable 360 camera approach places a portable camera on a stand and multiple exposures are taken, shooting with a DSLR involves:

1. Mounting your camera onto a panorama head on your tripod (in portrait orientation).

2. Taking four rotational images at 90° apart.

3. Taking one zenith shot (straight up).

4. Taking an optional nadir shot (straight down). I usually skip this, for reasons I'll mention throughout the book.

If you are photographing an interior you can optionally use flash, applying the flash-ambient technique and window pulls like you would with other interior work — but you don't have to. I will show how to shoot 360 panos using a DSLR with and without flash. If though you've been shooting interior real estate photography using the flash-ambient technique that I show in my videos and interiors book, then most of the flash-related steps will be familiar to you, except that you apply flash-ambient (and possibly window pulls) to each of the various shots of the pano (the four rotational, zenith, and optional nadir shots).

Whether shooting exteriors or interiors (with or without flash), the one difference compared to standard photography is the use of a panorama tripod head (recall I have recommendations for those in the "Pano Head" section of the "Gear" chapter). Here I'll assume you have the necessary gear outlined in the "DSLR Gear" section earlier in the book, and you're ready now to set it up.

Camera Mounting

Your pano head should be mounted as shown in the diagram below with the camera pointing forward in portrait orientation.

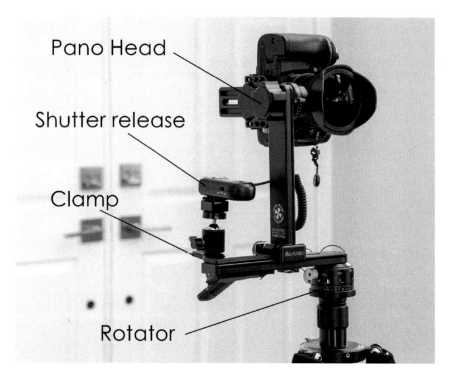

You may recall this image earlier in the "DSLR Gear" section, which has links to this gear (and more).

Nodal Ninja (the maker of this particular pano head) has a no-audio CAD-drawn video on the steps involved to mount your camera on their pano heads (similar to other pano heads) at this link:

youtube.com/watch?v=YT9eJhikPnc

…which also includes how to adjust the head for the parallax error, which I'll get to next. For now, the video segment from 0-2 minutes shows the camera mounting (2 minutes onward shows adjustments we'll get to shortly).

There are other ways to mount your camera on these pano heads to capture 360 panos, including an angled approach, which requires many more shots be taken.[26] That angled approach is more

---

[26] See video at youtube.com/watch?v=8uVJzyoTkd8

ideal for lenses that don't have a wide focal length. But since we use fisheye lenses to capture 360 panos for real estate, you only need to use the much simpler 4-around-1-up technique, so that's what this mounting (and the rest of the book) assumes you'll be doing.

Initial Setup (parallax calibration)

Since the process of shooting 360 panos with a DLSR requires you to rotate your camera on the pano head between multiple shots, your camera needs to ensure it doesn't change how distant and near objects line up from one shot to the next, something known as a *parallax error*. It's an easy thing to fix, and you only need to do this once when you initially setup your pano head for your particular DSLR and lens. This is one of those things you don't have to worry about in most other genres of photography, so if the term "parallax error" is foreign and has you squirming with anxiety, don't worry; it's simpler than it sounds. Let's first take a look at what a parallax error is, and then how you adjust your pano head for it.

First, after mounting your camera on you pano head, line up two objects: one near the camera and the other farther away. In the example below I placed a light stand near the camera, lining-up the top of the light stand with the crease/fold in the trifold screen in the distance. The alignment is circled in red.

Notice how the top of the light stand is aligned with that crease/fold in the trifold screen in the distance.

Next, using live view on the back of your camera, rotate the pano head to the right and again to the left; if you have no parallax error (which rarely happens on the initial setup), then you'd see that the near object (light stand) still lines up with the far object (the crease/fold in the trifold screen), as shown in these next two shots.

These show no parallax error, meaning the camera is mounted properly at the "no parallax point" on the pano head. When you first setup a camera-lens combo on a pano head though, there will inevitably be some kind of parallax error, like this:

Notice how the near and far images no longer align (the top of the light stand doesn't align with the crease in the trifold screen in the distance). To fix it, you need to do two things with your camera mounted on the pano head:

1. Point your camera straight down, and using live view make sure the center rotation point of the pano head is in the center of the frame, like so:

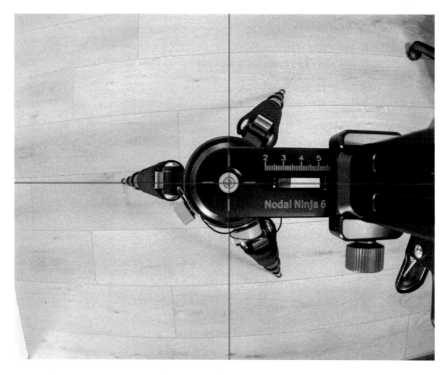

2. If not, move the pano head's vertical arm across its horizontal arm until you see this is centered. The horizontal arm is what I clamped the shutter release to in that shot above. Nodal Ninja has a lock so you can lock this in place once you are centered.

3. Rotate your camera back up so that it's pointing forward.

4. Move your camera forward or backward on the pano head's upper rail/arm by loosening the camera-mount knob; moving your camera slightly in one direction; and then tightening the camera-mount knob. **DO NOT TAKE YOUR HAND OFF YOUR CAMERA** when you loosen the camera-mount knob. Only remove your hand from your camera when the camera-mount knob is tight and secure.

Camera mount knob

5. Rotate the pano head again from left to right and see if you get a parallax error. If the parallax error is worse, then move the camera in the opposite direction that you did in step 4. In other words, if you moved your camera forward and now the parallax error is wider, then you need to move your camera slightly back.

6. Repeat steps 4 and 5 until there is no parallax error.

7. Set the lock on this arm to this position (if your camera has a lock).

Many good pano heads, like the Nodal Ninja 6, have locks (called "rail stops" on their diagrams[27]) that allow you to position the pano head arms to your no-parallax-point so that you never have to do this calibration again. Some pano heads also have a ruler/scale on the side so that you can write down (or take a

---

[27] See https://www.nodalninja.com/Manuals/NN6-QRG.pdf

cellphone pic) of where the adjustment is on each arm for the no-parallax-point.

In either case, this is a one-time step; however, if you change lenses or camera bodies, then you need to find its new no-parallax-point. I keep a lens permanently mounted on a camera body mainly for this reason — it's my permanent pano setup.

Footage Overview

There are five required and one optional shots for creating a 360 pano with a DSLR:

1. A shot with the pano head at 0°

2. A shot with the pano head at 90°

3. A shot with the pano head at 180°

4. A shot with the pano head at 270°

5. A zenith shot (with the camera looking straight up

6. An optional nadir (which I usually skip and just patch)

Shots 1-4 are what I call the "rotational" shots, taken with your camera in portrait orientation, as shown earlier like this:

The first shot is taken with the pano head's rotator at 0°, as shown in the inset in the picture above. After taking that first shot, you rotate to 90° to take the next shot, then rotate to 180° for the third shot, and rotate to 270° for the last rotational shot.

Shooting the zenith (shot #5) can be done at the last, 270° rotation, although I like to rotate back to 0°; either way, you just rotate the camera up, like so:

Then, if you really, really, *really*, want to shoot a nadir, you point the camera down, but by moving it across the pano arm after moving your tripod, like this (which not all pano heads can do):

I'll revisit these shots again in more detail later in this chapter when I get to the section showing the most involved way to shoot interior panos, with flash. Being the most complex method for interior panos, I made that section a superset of all the others in this chapter, so it has a lot more detail on all the steps involved. For now, we'll take simpler steps before diving into all of that.

While you can merely take one shot of each of these positions, like when capturing an exterior, when it comes to interior panos I shoot up to three frames for each of these positions since I like to incorporate flash in my 360 panos. You don't have to use flash, so I'll cover both ways in this chapter. If using flash, these shots are similar to the flash-ambient blending with darken-mode window pulls outlined in my interiors book, which are:

1. Ambient shot. No different from any other interior ambient shot, making sure your histogram is just right of center.[28] This is taken whether you use flash or not.

2. *Minor* flash shot. This is where things differ from regular interior flash photography. Since we use fisheye lenses for 360 panos, it's difficult to hide flash blooms. And you don't want to waste time trying to light every room that will fall in view, since, unlike regular interior photography, *every* room falls in view when you're shooting a 360 pano. Instead, there's an acceptable balance that will get you proper colors/white balance using *some* flash, without having to fuss with all of the other techniques of using flash for regular interior work.

3. Window pull shot(s) (optional). This is pretty much the same as you would do for regular interior flash work using the darken-mode window pull technique.[29] However, the difference for 360 panos is that you have to do window pulls for every positional shot that includes a portion of a window you want to pull. Since we're shooting 5 images minimum (4 around 1 up), many will overlap on the windows, including the zenith shot.

The first shot (ambient) is taken no matter what you're shooting (exteriors, interior with flash or without flash). Shots #2 and #3 are only if using flash for interiors, and are a bit more involved. To keep things simple, let's first walk through the steps of shooting exterior footage, which doesn't require any flash. After that, I'll step through shooting interior footage, at first not using flash, and then using flash.

Shooting Exterior Footage

Shooting exterior 360 panos with a DSLR is straightforward as no flash is involved. I recommend trying this first before moving on to interiors. Below is a link to the example pano I'll use here:

virtual-tour-book.remotehomeshowings.com/exterior-example-1

---

[28] See histogram video at: youtu.be/OTGFG9uWUUI?t=207
[29] See window pull video at: youtu.be/1Xmwr92n3GA

Here are the steps:

1. Level your tripod. It doesn't have to be exact, but it should be close. Use either the bubble level on your pano head or virtual horizon in live view.

2. Set your focus to infinity. Since most fisheye lenses are manual-focus lenses this can be an easy step to forget. It's very important though since you could have touched the focus ring on the lens when moving your camera from scene to scene.

3. Set the exposure using all manual settings. We only need one exposure setting for exterior 360 panos. I like to use the following settings for exterior shots on sunny days, even for regular exterior work:

    - ISO 200

    - f/8

    - 1/500 sec

    - WB = 5,500 K

    This gives me a fast enough shutter speed to shoot handheld, but since we're using a tripod for our 360 panos you could also use these settings:

    - ISO 100

    - f/8

    - 1/250 sec

    - WB = 5,500 K

    With high-ISO cameras nowadays there's little to no difference, and since I have these numbers burned into my brain I just opt for my go-to: ISO 200, f/8, 1/500 (and I always use fixed Kelvin outdoors). If you're not shooting on a sunny day though, you may want to adjust those settings a stop or so brighter, and optionally adjust your white balance as well. Same goes for twilights: if you shoot a 360 pano at twilight then use the exposure settings best suited for those conditions. Either way, make sure you are not using anything auto as you want all of your footage to have the same, consistent results for stitching (use manual white balance and all exposure settings manual too).

4. With the camera pointing straight ahead, shoot the four rotational shots at 90° apart (0°, 90°, 180°, 270°).

5. Rotate your pano head back to 0°, tilt your camera straight up, crouch down, and take the zenith shot.

6. Shoot the optional nadir (I usually skip that).

Here are the 5 shots used in this example:

The top three images and the one on the bottom left are the four rotational images, each shot at 90° apart. The other image (bottom right) is the zenith shot, with the camera pointing straight up. I like to rotate my pano head back to 0° for the zenith shot, which also has the pano head rotated for the next scene I'll shoot.

That's all there is to it. These five shots will then be stitched together later to create a 360 pano. I'll be covering those steps in the "DSLR Workflow" section of the "Editing Workflows" chapter, with additional steps in the "PTGui Primer" chapter.

Shooting Interiors with no Flash

I prefer to shoot my DSLR 360 panos using flash, but that can be a big step if you're new to using a DSLR for 360 panos, and/or using flash in general. So while the next section will show how to use flash when shooting 360 panos, this section is simplified using no flash, just ambient. Although this simpler, no-flash option is a stepping-stone to using flash, this ambient-only approach will often result in better quality than using a portable 360 camera, so it's more than just practice; it's also practical (at times).

Since this procedure is almost identical to shooting an exterior 360 pano with a DSLR, I'll merely list the steps. These steps should be familiar to you if you've gone through the last section on shooting exteriors, but there are some differences, namely in exposure and white balance.

Here are the steps:

1. Level your tripod. It doesn't have to be exact, but it should be close.

2. Set your focus to infinity.

3. Set the white balance to auto.

4. Set the exposure. We only need one exposure setting for exterior 360 panos, which needs to be consistent across all of the four rotational shots, zenith, and optional nadir. I prefer to use ISO 320, f/7.1, and then adjust the shutter speed until the histogram is measuring right of center, just like you would do when shooting any interior ambient shots. Many times the shutter speed is around 1/10 second, but you need to find the most optimum shutter speed for your pano, usually best decided from the most feature-rich shot of the pano (making sure the histogram measures right of center for that particular shot).

5. Shoot the four rotational shots at 90° apart, and one zenith (and optional nadir).

These five shots will then be stitched together later to create a 360 pano. I'll be covering those steps in the "DSLR Workflow" section of the "Editing Workflows" chapter, with additional steps in the "PTGui Primer" chapter.

Shooting Interiors with Flash

Assuming you're using flash for your DSLR 360 panos, this section covers the steps involved. I also dedicated a chapter, "Using Flash" to cover techniques you can use if you want to incorporate flash into your 360 panos. Here though we'll walk through the steps to photograph a 360 pano with flash, using an example I hosted at the link below.

virtual-tour-book.RemoteHomeShowings.com/example-dslr-family-dining

You can also see the difference between this example (shot with a DSLR using flash) and another using the Ricoh Theta Z1 at this link:

virtual-tour-book.remotehomeshowings.com/dslr-vs-thetaz1-examples

As we step through the process of gathering the footage for this pano you can refer to the image below, which shows the three frames we'll take (ambient, flash, window pull) at each position (four around, one up) and the blended image for one of the rotational shots comprising that 360 pano:

ISO 320, f/7.1

Ambient
1/20 sec

Flash
1/80 sec

Window Pull
1/160 sec

Blended
Image

By looking at the ambient shot it becomes obvious why you might want to use flash for this pano. But bear in mind that although this shows the blended image (flash-ambient blended with the darken-mode window pull) this is not a finished product. We'll be touching things up after the pano is stitched. This is merely our starting point.

Since shooting interior 360 panos with flash is more involved than the ambient-only methods covered so far, I wrote the steps here as subsections to give you more *whys* behind the *hows* that you can later navigate to more easily from the table of contents. Here are the steps.

Prepare your flash

Make sure to have your flash trigger mounted in the hot-shoe of your camera and turn it on. You'll want to leave this trigger turned on throughout the entire process with the channel activated that matches the flash unit you'll be using. You don't want to mess with your trigger while it's mounted on your camera; you'll only use one flash unit, handheld, turned on as needed, adjusting its power manually (see the "Using Flash" chapter if you want to read more as to why).

Level your tripod

It doesn't have to be exact, but you should be fairly level. You can use the bubble level on your pano head, or virtual horizon in live view on your camera.

Set your focus

Usually this is set to infinity on most fisheye lenses. It's something to remember in your steps of shooting a 360 pano since most fisheye lenses are manual-focus lenses. When you move your camera to the next scene, you may have touched your lens casing, which I sometimes do when putting the lens cap back on, and it could have moved the lens's focus ring. If you're like me and you get used to using autofocus, this seemingly simple step can be hard to remember. It's also good to know where your lens's infinity is, since each lens is slightly different. Many fisheye lenses like the Samyang 12mm f/2.8 for Nikon, also have an AE chip to confirm focus.

Find the starting angle

It's best to decide where to begin your rotation. Unlike the exterior and no-flash methods, we need to optimize how we'll use flash in the scene; namely, where windows will fall between rotational shots. The living room/dining room combo space in our example has multiple windows that I'd like to pull (using the darken-mode window pull technique), but there are some that I don't want to pull (facing the neighbor's house). So it's best to find a good starting point/angle so that you can minimize (or eliminate) the need to do overlapping window pulls between the four rotational shots. I like to use my tripod's center column for this so that I only use my pano head's rotator for rotating between each rotated shot — not for setting it up. This allows me to keep my zero position on the rotator where I want it, not where I have to compose. It's a preference, but I find that by first finding the best starting point to begin my rotation, my flashing and editing goes smoother.

Below is a shot of the pano head's rotator at zero.

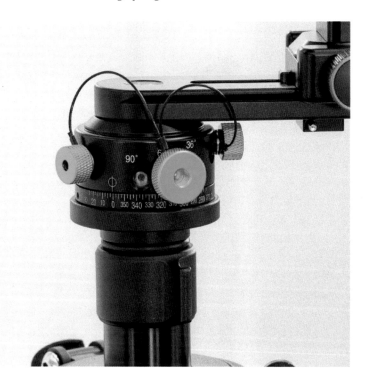

Set the white balance

As with all other interior photography, I recommend setting your camera's white balance to auto. The same goes for portable 360 cameras, but the advantage of using a DSLR with flash is that our flash shots will almost always have correct white balance — or something very close to it — when the camera is set to auto white balance and we fire a flash. This will become more obvious as we set the exposure settings (next step) since the goal of each flashed shot is to dominate the white balance to obtain more correct colors than ambient alone. Note though that some flash triggers can cause auto white balance issues for any kind of interior photography, something you may recall earlier in the book when talking about gear for DSLRs.[30]

---

[30] Watch my video on this at https://youtu.be/RCQO24hcjMo

Determine your exposure settings

Before shooting your footage, you need to determine what exposure settings you'll be using, since you need to use the same exposure settings for all of the four rotational shots, the zenith shot, and the optional nadir. Here's how I do it:

1. Take an ambient test shot at the most important, feature-rich area of the pano. In the example for this section I opted for the view to the backyard through the dining room. Whatever you choose, this is the most important area so we want to make sure it gets the most attention, and hence best exposure, since this will likely be the initial view when the pano is hosted. Find a good exposure so that your histogram measures just right of center. You can start with the same exposure settings I talk about in my other books for interior photography: ISO 320, f/7.1, and then adjust your shutter speed until your histogram is right of center after taking a shot. Remember the shutter speed.

2. Increase the shutter speed by two stops. That's usually six clicks on most shutter wheel dials since most cameras adjust exposure in 1/3-stop increments. Fire your flash and adjust flash power until you see a flash power setting that looks decent enough. Don't try to get fancy; we just want to make sure we're getting proper color and not under- or over-exposing too much. Remember the shutter speed and the flash power.

3. Determine your shutter speed and flash power for your window pulls. This is the same as step #2, except you're ensuring that you have enough (but not too much) flash power for the window pull with an exposure that gives you the outside view you want. As with interior photography, this is often 1/160 second (at the same ISO 320 f/7.1 used for the other shots). Remember the shutter speed and the flash power.

   a. If you're shooting a million-dollar view and you find that you need to lower the ISO (say to 200 or even 100) to get a clear view to the outside, then consider going back to steps #1 and #2 to reevaluate your settings using that lower ISO. There's enough to remember with just the shutter speeds and flash power settings, so it's best to try to use a constant ISO and aperture for all of the shots for a 360 pano. Also, fisheye lenses tend to let in a lot more light than other lenses you may be using for regular interior photography, so you may find that you can squeeze enough power out of your flash unit to easily satisfy an ISO 200.

At this point there's a lot to remember, especially since you'll need to recall settings while also remembering to rotate from 0-90, 90-180, 180-270, and 270-0 on the pano head (and don't forget the zenith). Your mind might be swimming with numbers, so at first you might want to jot down the exposure and flash settings on a post-it note and stick it to your camera or tripod (keep a pen and post-its in your back pocket, for instance).

The hard part is now over, so you can relax and take a deep breath. As you do, take a moment to remember how far you've come. You've proven you can shoot real estate photography and learned skills you didn't have before. Shooting 360 panos with a DSLR is just another *new* skill. You learned new photography skills in the past, so you know you can do it again. Be patient with yourself. You can do this. It may take time, but don't give up! Remember: a quitter never wins, and a winner never quits. When you encounter problems, welcome them. They will strengthen your understanding and make you a better photographer.

Shoot the rotational shots

Now that you know your exposure and flash settings, you can start shooting. I often take a shot with my hand in front of the camera to know this is where I started shooting the pano (knowing that shots before it were just testers). The steps for the four rotational shots are as follows:

1. Turn the flash trigger on in your camera's hot-shoe and leave it on for all of these steps.

2. Turn off your flash unit (I usually have mine in my back pocket or clipped to my belt).

3. Set your pano head to 0° (the starting point you determined earlier).

4. Set your camera's ambient exposure settings to what you determined in the last section.

5. Take the ambient shot.

6. Change the shutter speed to the flash exposure you determined in the last section.

7. Turn on your flash unit.

8. Hold your flash just above your head facing up, about 1-2' behind you.

9. Take the flash shot.

10. If you are shooting a window pull, then change the camera's shutter speed to that setting and fire that shot (with the flash pointed at the window).

    a. As with window pulls for standard interior photography, I also often take a no-flash window pull shot in case I need to use it to patch things in post.[31] I always take those no-flash window pull shots for big picture windows with views.

11. Turn off your flash unit.

12. Rotate your pano head to the next position.

13. Repeat steps 4-12 for the other 3 rotational shots.

---

[31] See video as well at https://youtu.be/W6Qvg_ZbqjU

Shoot the zenith

Shooting the zenith is very similar to shooting the four rotational shots, except that you point your camera up, like so:

Here are the steps.

1. Make sure the flash trigger is still on in your camera's hot shoe.

2. Turn off your flash unit (it should be off from step 11 in the last section).

3. Set your pano head to rotation 0°.

4. Rotate your camera straight up.

5. Set your camera's ambient exposure to the same as what you used for your rotational shots.

6. Crouch down, out of view.

7. Take the ambient shot.

8. Change the shutter speed to the flash exposure.

9. Turn on your flash unit.

10. Crouch down, out of view.

11. Point your flash at the floor or low on a wall, preferably at something white or light colored.

12. Take the flash shot.

13. If you are shooting a window pull, then change the camera's shutter speed to that setting and fire that shot.

14. Stand back up.

15. Rotate the camera back to where it was, pointing straight forward.

Shooting the Nadir (optional)

As I mentioned earlier, I rarely shoot the nadir. It's usually not worth the time to shoot, it takes additional edits, and if all else fails you can patch it (more on that in the "Nadir Patching" section in the "Editing Workflows" chapter). If though you want to include a *real* nadir, using the Nodal Ninja 6 with the Nadir Adapter you can move your camera over the nadir spot without getting too much of your tripod in the shot like this:

As this photo shows, the Nodal Ninja 6 allows you to spin the vertical pano head arm 180° and slide it to the end, allowing your camera to extend out over the edge of the tripod; then, you also need to move your tripod so that the camera is pointing at the approximate point where all the other shots were taken. That's often a crapshoot, but you can make it work if you really want to. If you want to see the Nodal Ninja nadir adapter in action, check out this video starting at 47 seconds:

https://youtu.be/vPEMsNv8kuw?t=47

For me though, I rarely do this, especially for standard real estate virtual tours. I never felt comfortable with the amount of "tip" from the tripod with the camera hanging out so far. And since I often have to edit *some* stuff out of the shot (part of my tripod is almost always in the nadir), I either leave a blank nadir in my panos or I do a nadir patch (more on that in the "Nadir Patching" section in the "DSLR Workflow").

Using Flash

If you are using a portable 360 camera, or not using flash with your DSLR for photographing 360 panos, then you can skip ahead to the "Software" chapter.

If you are using a DSLR for shooting 360 panos and you want to incorporate flash for high-end results, this chapter will elaborate on the flash-ambient and window-pull flash techniques shown in the "Shooting Interiors with Flash" section of the last chapter, and how this will apply to the DSLR Workflow later in the book. To keep the upcoming workflow chapter concise, I'll elaborate on using flash here in this chapter and refer back to it as needed throughout the book. I do though recommend going through this chapter now as it will help to set the foundation for understanding how flash will be used throughout the entire process. The process is similar to using flash for other interior work — which I cover in some of my other books — but there are some differences.

The Principles for Flash

Using flash for photographing 360 pano footage with a DSLR is simpler than that for other interior work. The goals of using flash for these panos are:

1. Get correct color. By using flash with a camera exposing just slightly above ambient, the flashed lighting will become the dominant white balance, and thus provide more accurate colors.

2. Reduce ambient artifacts. We don't want to eliminate all ambient light since this would require such a low exposure that we'd lose the benefit of capturing correct colors; in other words, we can't use such a dark exposure that we

can't see any ambient light (no light, no color). Flash is not intended to replace ambient light; it's only to dominate the white balance and reduce glare.

3. Optional window pulls, allowing you to capture clear views to the outside.

Remember that by using any level of flash you'll have better results than if you just used a portable 360 camera, or a DSLR with no flash. It's not feasible to use flash to its full extent for shooting the footage for a DSLR 360 pano since it would not only take a lot longer to properly flash the five minimum shots for a 360 pano with fancy lighting, but your fisheye lens will inevitably capture flash blooms, and we need to ensure that each of the five shots are as natural as possible for the stitching process. Take for instance these four flash shots (for each rotation), which were used for this particular 360 pano:

virtual-tour-book.remotehomeshowings.com/flash-principle-example

These would typically not be acceptable for standard interior work, but they meet the goals for what we'll need for a 360 pano, using a special take on the flash-ambient blend technique.

I'll elaborate later in this chapter, but the main reason is that we'll use a simple flash-ambient blend that uses the *entire* ambient layer (in Luminosity blending mode) with layer opacity between 60-70%. Most everything we want to do when it comes to editing 360 panos is to make global edits, which help to ensure seamless stitching. By applying a global flash-ambient blend instead of painting ambient selectively (like I show in the interiors book), not only is the workflow faster, but flashing is greatly simplified.

Flash Gear

While I discussed flash gear earlier in the book, I want to elaborate on it here for its applicability at this point in the process. Since we're capturing such large areas photographing footage for a 360 pano with a DSLR, you will likely only want to use one flash unit and not keep it on a light stand. I like to use the AD200Pro since it has enough power for most spaces in almost any situation and I can put it in my back pocket. When I do flashed shots for a 360 pano, the flash is minimal, so keeping the flash at the ready in my pocket helps things move quickly.

Another option to keep your flash with you, if you are using an AD200Pro, is to use a belt clip with a standard 1/4" screw that can attach to the AD200 like this one:

https://amzn.to/3gCfeHX

Besides the clip and flash, you may also want to consider an omnidirectional diffuser, like the MagMod Sphere:

https://amzn.to/3gBdkYa

You can't slide your AD200 into your pocket easily with this attached, but it would work well if you use a belt clip.

Flash Position

Flashing a 360 pano is best done handheld so that you can capture all of your 360 shots (four rotational, zenith, and optional nadir) quickly. You don't want to be fiddling with stands, which can get in the way when working in tight spaces with a fisheye lens. In any case, your flash position is very simple for shooting flashed shots for your 360 panos: just hold the flash pointing up near or slightly above your head, tilted back slightly. This will help to reduce light bloom on the ceiling. Remember that we're not out for anything fancy, which is evident by those four flash shots I showed at the beginning of this chapter.

Window Pulls

Shooting window pulls for regular interior photos and for 360 panos is similar, but there are slight differences. Take these three window pull shots that were part of the example I showed earlier in this chapter.

Pointing the flash directly at the windows with the camera exposing for the outdoors gets us a darken-mode window pull shot, just like I show in the interiors book. And, since there were a number of windows, I flashed two window pull shots on that far wall during one rotational position. So far so good; it's the same as we'd do for regular interior photography. The third shot though was necessary and could have easily been overlooked. In that third shot we can see a small sliver of the sliding door in the distance, which needed a window pull so that the finished shot would stitch properly across the overlapping regions of these shots (I'll cover more on stitching in the "Editing Workflows" chapter). These tiny slivers of windows show up not only in the rotational shots, but also sometimes in the zenith, so make sure to flash for window pulls in that shot too.

Once again, you can see the finished pano with these window pulls at:

virtual-tour-book.remotehomeshowings.com/flash-principle-example

Flash-Ambient Blending

At the heart of using flash for 360 panos with a DSLR is the flash-ambient blend process using a variant of the 50-50 technique, similar to what I show in this video:

https://www.youtube.com/watch?v=SgicG9VtHf4

I'll step through an example here, which will use the following high-level steps you may already be familiar with from my interiors book and videos:

1. Turn the ambient layer into Luminosity blending mode.

2. Change the ambient layer's opacity to 60% or 70%.

3. Optionally apply darken-mode window pulls.

Although the upcoming example shows these steps, if this so far is unfamiliar to you then I'd encourage you to first work through my book on interior real estate photography, which will show much more detail to these steps, as well as the reasons and principles behind them.

Example

The following steps in this example are a variant of the flash-ambient blend technique from my interiors book, using one of the four rotational shots for the example 360 pano shown earlier in this chapter. The main difference in the technique shown here and work you do for other real estate photography using flash-ambient, is that the ambient layer (in Luminosity blending mode) does *not* have a layer mask; instead the ambient layer's opacity is lowered, thereby providing its luminance in its entirety (not selectively painted on), controlled to a global degree (through the percentage of layer opacity). This method is important to keep footage consistent for the stitching process, which each of these shots will be used for later in the workflow. For now, here are the steps to apply this kind of flash-ambient blend (with darken-mode window pulls).

1. Load all layers into Photoshop from Lightroom as you would any other flash-ambient blended image. When you do, you should have something that looks like the screenshot below. Note there were two window pull shots for this example, which is sometimes the case in such wide shots using a fisheye lens for shooting 360 panos.

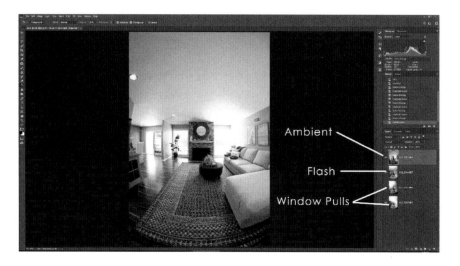

2. Select the ambient layer.

3. Set the ambient layer's blending mode to Luminosity.

4. Set the ambient layer's opacity to 60%. You should now see something like this:

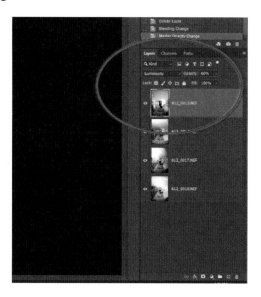

5. If this doesn't look like enough ambient, then change the opacity to 70% or 80%. Conversely, if there was too much ambient then change the layer opacity to 50% or 40%.

Remember though that whatever opacity percentage you choose in this first image, it must be the same for the other rotational shots, zenith, and optional nadir.

6. If you don't have any window pulls, then skip to step 9.

7. Add the optional window pulls by dragging them one by one to the top; change the layer blending mode to Darken; and add a hide-all layer mask to each window pull layer. Since we had two window pulls for this shot, it should now look like this with those two window pulls at the top (note the blending mode is Darken and each has a hide-all layer mask):

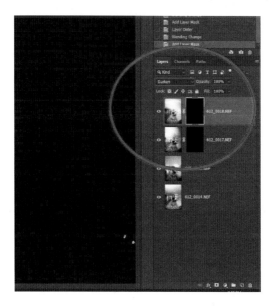

8. With the mask selected, either paint using a brush or select with the polygon tool the windows on the image, just like you would do for any other window pull. After you do you'll see something like the screenshot below with white areas on the mask where the windows are in the image and with a clear view to the outside through the windows:

9. Flatten the image and save it. It will now be loaded back into Lightroom.

10. In Lightroom, export this image as a 16-bit TIFF, retaining all Metadata (we'll cover this later in the workflow later in the book). Don't do any more editing yet; just export it as a TIFF.

11. Repeat this process for the other three rotational shots, the zenith, and optional nadir. But, make sure to use the same layer opacity percentage for your ambient layer that you did for the first image (steps #4 and #5).

    This example was one of many steps in the DSLR editing workflow. I'll discuss when to implement this technique in the workflow in the "DSLR Workflow" section of the "Editing Workflows" chapter.

Software

This chapter serves as a preparation for the workflows we'll cover in the next chapter by first discussing the software for editing. By knowing the *whys* (in this chapter) before the *whats* (in the next chapter), this chapter can give you broader insight into the concepts and tools needed for editing almost any 360 pano from almost any camera.

Lightroom and Photoshop

As you may recall from the Introduction chapter, this book assumes you have at least a basic understanding of using Adobe's Lightroom and Photoshop programs. Like other pro photography work, these two programs are de facto industry standards, crucial to editing workflows. In particular, if using Adobe products, you'll want to use Lightroom Classic (not just Lightroom, which is a scaled down version), and Photoshop. You can get both for a $10/month subscription from Adobe under their Photograph Plan.

I get asked occasionally if there are other programs besides Adobe products that can be used for pro photography editing, and there are; however, Adobe products are widely used in this industry and fit well in professional photography workflows, so that's what I'll be using here. If you need help coming up to speed on Lightroom and Photoshop, I would suggest taking a look at my Advanced Editing Guide for Real Estate, in particular the chapter on working with layers and masks. Also, if you aren't familiar with the real estate photography editing workflow, then I would also suggest taking a look at my book on interior photography.

While Lightroom and Photoshop are important tools for virtual tours, the most critical program for 360-photography is known as a "stitcher": a software program that creates the 360 pano from the footage you shot. What stitcher you use will depend on what camera you're using to photograph your virtual tours. First I'll cover some of the portable 360° camera stitchers, and then options for stitching 360 panos shot with a DSLR.

Stitchers for Portable Cameras

Almost every manufacturer of portable 360° cameras provides free stitching software that blends the fisheye images taken from their cameras into a seamless 360 pano. Although each portable 360 camera manufacturer provides their own stitching software, you can use a universal stitching program like PTGui, which is mainly used for stitching DSLR images into a 360 pano.

In the next chapter when we get to the workflows, I'll cover the steps involved using the various stitching programs. Here though I'd like to briefly discuss the stitching software for the portable 360° cameras I've covered so far.

In short: For portable cameras, Ricoh provides the best stitching software for the pro editing workflow. QooCam is difficult and Insta360 isn't much better. Since Ricoh tops the list for portable 360 cameras here — in quality and workflow — I'll spend the most time in this chapter discussing it, and how to set it up for your workflow.

Note that stitching 360 panos from a DSLR can sometimes be simpler. That's how we'll end this chapter.

Ricoh

Ricoh provides a stitching plugin for Adobe Lightroom, which you can download from their support download page.[32] Once you download and install this app/plugin, they have documentation that — as is too often the case with these portable 360 cameras — is rather poor. But, in a subdirectory called

---

[32] support.theta360.com/en/download

"manual" they provide PDFs with instructions to install their stitcher to integrate with Lightroom (launched when you export an image).

To make things easier, I recommend installing the Ricoh stitcher (and all stitchers, in fact) in a directory of your choosing, not the default which is sometimes buried deep some place like under Window's "Program Files" directory structure. You will need to find things in their install directories, so I recommend putting this into something easy to find, like on Windows just C:\Ricoh.

Once you install the Ricoh Theta Stitcher, the instructions to integrate it with Lightroom are fairly straightforward, but the use of it is poorly documented. I'll square that away here, assuming you have already installed the Ricoh Theta Stitcher installed:

1. Launch Lightroom.

2. From the menu, select Edit >> Preferences.

3. Select the "External Editing" tab.

4. Under "Additional External Editor", click the "Choose" button and navigate to where you installed the Ricoh Theta Stitcher, and select the program, which on Windows is called "RICOH THETA Stitcher.exe".

5. Save this as a preset by selecting under the "Preset" dropdown "Save Current Settings as Preset", and enter "RICOH THETA Stitcher" for the preset name, and click Create".

6. Here's a screen shot of the Preferences dialog. If everything looks like so, then click OK.

While that is a one-time process, you will need to select that Ricoh preset when you export images from Lightroom. I'll cover that in the "Editing Workflows" chapter, but here is a screenshot of what the Lightroom export dialog should look like when you export using the stitcher:

Ricoh's stitcher is not flexible when it comes to file naming and directory structures, so you need to make sure that you:

- Export To: Same folder as original photo

- Rename To: Filename – Sequence

- Image Format: TIFF, sRGB, 16 bit (necessary for editing later)

- Metadata: All Metadata (necessary to retain EXIF used by stitchers and many 360 hosts)

- Post-Processing, After Export: Open in RICOH THETA Stitcher.exe

After you click "Export" on Lightroom's export dialog, and once Lightroom creates the exported TIFF, it will then bring up the Ricoh stitcher, like this:

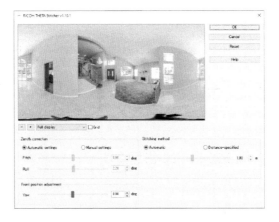

You just click OK and it will create a stitched image (in this case we are using TIFF format).

QooCam

QooCam's stitching software, QooCam Studio[33], is somewhat lacking. For instance, even though you can shoot in

RAW format with the QooCam 8K 360 camera, their QooCam Studio program can't load a RAW file shot with their cameras, which makes no sense. Instead, to make their software work with the maximum editing flexibility in the workflows, you can use the QooCam Studio software as the very last step, loading in a TIFF file to be stitched; however, QooCam Studio expects the image orientation to be as it was taken out of the camera — vertical, like this:

---

[33] https://www.kandaovr.com/download

This is a terrible orientation for editing since monitors are wide, not tall. To make things easier, when I show the steps for the QooCam workflow I've included steps to rotate images at different times, making it easier to edit while still making it compatible with QooCam Studio.

Using QooCam Studio is rather straightforward: you just enter their "Edit" screen by clicking on "Edit".

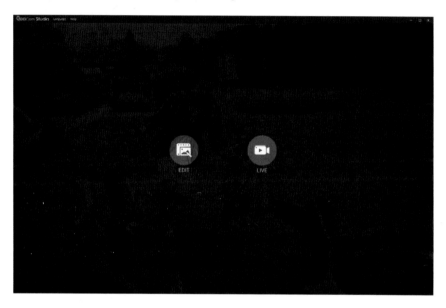

Then, you can either drop and drag or click the "Add" button to add your image (in the workflows that will be your final TIFF).

There is a "Render" button on the bottom right that you click, which then allows you to render this as a JPG.

Note that I had one heck of a time getting QooCam images to work well with PTGui; however, PTGui does seem to stitch the QooCam DNG files well. But stitching before exposure blending (part of the workflow I'll get to in the next chapter) could cause layer misalignment, so the use of PTGui with QooCam images is subject to problems; thus I won't use PTGui in the QooCam workflow.

Insta360

Insta360 provides a program called Insta360 Studio[34] for stitching, but it doesn't work well in the pro editing workflow, mainly since this software can't load a TIFF file, only JPGs or DNG RAW files. This complicates the workflow since you can't stitch a TIFF at the very end like you would with the Ricoh and QooCam. Instead, you could stitch all of your DNG files first and then edit them as layers using Lightroom and Photoshop, but doing this risks layer misalignment later when you do exposure blending (something I'll get into in the workflow chapter). Because of this I don't recommend the use of Insta360 Studio in the workflow; instead, I'll recommend using PTGui as the stitching program at the very end of the workflow, which allows you to load a TIFF file for stitching. Unlike QooCam, I was able to successfully use PTGui for the Insta360 workflow.

Stitchers for DSLRs

Stitching a 360 pano from shots taken with a DSLR can sometimes be simpler than the process of using a portable 360 camera, and it's far more powerful. But being powerful and flexible means there are cases that could be more complex. After a short learning curve I'm sure you'll find it streamlined and flexible. Moreover though, stitching DSLR photos is the same workflow no matter what camera you are using. This is a huge benefit to pro photography work as you don't have to continually fiddle with new software releases, or the annoying nuances between the various portable 360 cameras you may have for your business.

---

[34] https://www.insta360.com/download/insta360-onex

Note that the stitching process for a DSLR is not the same as creating a pano using Photoshop's Photomerge tool. Stitching a 360° panorama creates a wrap-around pano with a clearly defined beginning and end, correcting fisheye distortion with corrected vertical lines. While there are tutorials online on how to use Photoshop to create a 360 pano, I find it's much faster and more accurate to use an inexpensive stitching program. Here I'll talk about two DSLR stitching programs I recommend, and a tempting free option I'd stay clear of.

PTGui

PTGui (ptgui.com) has been the gold standard for stitching 360 panos. Being a universal stitcher, not only can it be used for stitching DLSR images into a 360 pano; you can also use it to stitch almost any 360 image into a pano (i.e. from Ricoh, Insta360, etc.). This makes PTGui universal, so it's something I highly recommend. PTGui costs about $140. It's a one-time cost, and there is a free version you can try as well. That small investment is more than worth what it provides.

Although there are other 360 pano stitchers out there, PTGui is the program I'll use throughout the rest of the book for working with DSLR panos. Still, there is one other contender worth mentioning, and definitely considering.

Panoweaver

If you want to try something different than PTGui, then Panoweaver[35] by Easypano is a stitching program that's definitely worth considering. Its Standard Edition is just slightly more than PTGui at $150, but its full-featured Pro edition costs $400. Easypano provides a free trial download so that you can see if this program may be to your liking. Among the various universal 360 stitchers I've worked with, Panoweaver rivals PTGui as its

---

[35] http://www.easypano.com/store-panoweaver.html

workflow is straightforward, and results were quite similar to PTGui as well. But, I still recommend PTGui over this program since PTGui is considered by many (including me) to be the gold standard for 360 image stitching. Nevertheless, I wouldn't discourage anyone from giving Panoweaver a try.

There are a few *different* things about Panoweaver to note, and since I'll only be covering the use of PTGui in the next chapter when outlining the workflow for DSLR panos, I thought I'd mention Panoweaver's basic steps here:

1. Open your images under the menu File >> Import Source Images

2. You may be prompted to define the image type, since Panoweaver doesn't seem to read all of the necessary EXIF data from TIFFs exported from Lightroom (a step covered in the workflows in the next chapter). Since I use a full-frame camera with a fisheye lens, that's what I select when prompted at this step.

3. Stich the images from the menu Panorama >> Stitch

4. Save the pano from the menu Panorama >> Save Panoramic Image

Not correctly reading EXIF from TIFFs in Panoweaver made this a bit annoying, and also made me suspicious of the program itself — the EXIF is indeed in the TIFF files to be stitched and PTGui has no problem interpreting them automatically. Nevertheless, the results using Panoweaver were very good. In fact, I found that Panoweaver did a slightly better job than PTGui at identifying "Matching Points" (PTGui calls these "Control Points") to define the points on overlapping images used in its stitching process. Granted, I only tested a few panos with Panoweaver, but the results were quite impressive.

Panoweaver is definitely a contender to consider, but for the rest of the book I will use PTGui. The principles though are basically the same. Easypano, the company that makes Panoweaver, also offers Tourweaver[36], a software package you can use to create virtual tours that you can self-host (similar to Marzipano).

Hugin

Hugin[37] is free stitching software that you may find in your search for 360 stitchers. Being free might entice you to try this out, but I would not recommend this program. While the mostly manual operations performed with Hugin can eventually provide you with a 360 pano, its higher effort compared to PTGui, the lack of decent documentation, and the poor workflow make this a program I would not recommend for pro work. I mention it in this book only to say, "Skip it." If you search the web then you're sure to find bloggers talking about this software, but since bloggers often talk without testing, I can honestly say that after doing *real* hands-on testing, I would not waste time working with it.

---

[36] https://www.easypano.com/virtual-tour-software.html
[37] http://hugin.sourceforge.net

Editing Workflows

This chapter contains two workflow sections for editing your 360 panos:

- Portable 360 Camera Workflows

- DSLR Workflow

The DSLR workflow is universal to almost any kind of DSLR. But the section on portable 360 cameras is more complex as it takes a lot more finessing to get professional results from these portable cameras, and each camera's software handles things differently. There is a quick and dirty way to edit portable 360 camera shots, and while I'll touch on that briefly in this chapter it's not the goal of this book. I realize the workflows in this chapter (especially for portable cameras) may seem arduous, but please bear in mind that my goal here is to show you the widest spectrum for the highest quality results that you can attain using any method of shooting 360 panos. Once you understand these workflows you might find compromises that can simplify your work. But I would encourage you to first go through the workflows in this chapter to get a broader understanding of the *whys* behind the *whats*, and the steps taken to get there.

Portable Camera Workflows

I have a love-hate relationship with using portable 360 cameras for virtual tours. I can usually get in and out of a property quicker using them versus a DSLR, but the editing can be painful to get results that are anything close to professional. But, it can be done — to some degree.

The Quick and Dirty

All 360° cameras can simply create JPG files, and many can produce an in-camera HDR JPG as well. If you're not familiar with Lightroom, Photoshop, or your market doesn't support the time and effort to produce higher quality images for your virtual tours, then the straight-to-jpg/HDR option may be something to consider, at least for the short term. This is not something I recommend, but if you have everything else down pat yet you're overwhelmed by the editing workflows, then a straight-to-jpg/HDR option could help you until you can get more 360 experience under your belt. So if all else fails, don't give up; just jpg it — but only temporarily. If you do take the quick-and-dirty, HDR/JPG route, then the rest of this chapter won't apply, so you can jump ahead to the "Hosting" chapter. I would though encourage you to at least try these workflows, and if you don't get them at first, don't get frustrated, just try and try again.

Exposure Blending

The portable 360 workflow steps in this chapter include a step called "Exposure Blending". It's a complicated kind of step, so instead of including how to do exposure blending for each kind of camera, this section will cover exposure blending generically, and in detail. It's something you can do with footage from any kind of portable 360 camera.

The purpose of exposure blending for portable 360 cameras is to reduce noise/grain and broaden the dynamic range. Portable 360 cameras are *notorious* for noise — way more noise than you get out of the cheapest DSLRs. Even using the Ricoh Theta Z1 with its big sensors with its low, ISO 80, there is a *ton* of noise in the shadows, even in their RAW files. This can greatly hinder the editing process to get pro results; however, if you fill in shadowed areas with higher exposed images, then the noise will be greatly reduced, and naturally. Exposure blending using luminosity masks in Photoshop helps to take care of that.

While I'll step through exposure blending in this section, I also have a YouTube video showing this technique at:

https://youtu.be/n5QtoSB4VOs

To see how and why exposure blending is done step by step, let's first take a look at an edited 360 image that used exposure blending, right before the stitching process:

That was a blend of five different images, each taken at a slightly different exposure (2/3 stop apart for each), which helped to broaden the dynamic range (lightening shadows while reducing highlights). Here are the shots that were exposure-blended to make that image:

Having an image that exposes for the shadows (the first image) and one that exposes for the outside view (the last image), shooting other exposures in between these two extremes allows us to selectively blend exposures from these various images to brighten the shadows with reduced noise, while obtaining *some* outside view. Exposure blending with luminosity masks helps us select areas of exposure in each shot that we want to fill in using the other shots. This is how it's done:

1. Load all of these images as layers into Photoshop. This is done the same way I show in the interiors book (and others) where you select multiple images in the Lightroom filmstrip, right click, and select "Open as Layers in Photoshop". When you go to Photoshop, you should then see something like this, where all of the images are layers in the layers panel (outlined in red in this screenshot):

2. I like to start shooting for the brightest exposure; hence, in this example the brightest exposure is on top and the darkest exposure is on the bottom. If you don't see your images in this order, I'd suggest arranging them so they are.

3. Starting at the top (brightest exposure) move the *next* exposure to the top. In this case, since we just started, we'd move layer #2 to the top. Then add a hide-all layer mask to this now-uppermost layer (you can select Layer >> Layer Mask >> Hide All from the menus). You should then see something like this:

4. Now select the layer directly below:

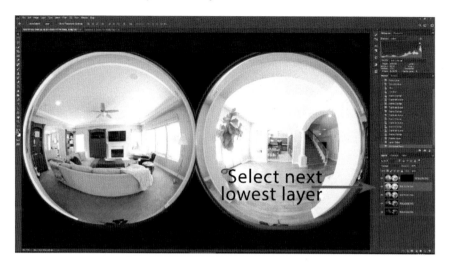

5. Now comes the tricky part. Select the Channels tab on the layers panel.

6. While holding down the CTRL key, click on the small icon on the RGB channel:

7. This will place "marching ants" (dashed outline) around the areas that measure highlights at or above 50% exposure. This is the key to luminosity masking: selecting areas based on luminosity/exposure.

8. Next, you will want to do what's called an *intersection*, which will refine how much of the highlighted area (the level of highlights) will be selected. You do this by doing CTRL+ALT+SHIFT+Click on that RGB icon. Each time you do that, you should see the selected area (defined by the marching ants) shrink. This refines your selection so that you can choose to leave or remove certain levels of highlights in the next steps. I find most often that one intersection (doing CTRL+ALT+SHIFT+Click once) is good for the first layer I'm working with, and then each layer/exposure after that requires more and more intersections to define those areas (by the time I'm doing the views I'm intersecting up to 10 times or more, but 3-5 times for most of the other layers).

9. Select the Layers tab on the Layers panel, and select the layer mask of the top layer:

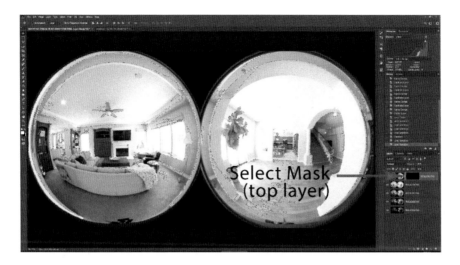

10. Now use a brush at a low to medium flow (30% flow works well), and brush over the bright areas on the image. You will see those highlights begin to darken while darker areas are less affected by your brush. It should start looking something like this:

11. Note the layer mask's black area (not brushed in) on the left lens and how that corresponds to the unselected area behind the couch. That area, as an example, was not selected during the luminosity masking steps (steps 5-8), because its highlights were low (that area was mostly shadow). While you could have

skipped those steps and just brushed this in manually, you would have inevitably overlapped into those dark areas, which we don't want to touch. Luminosity masking protected those darker areas.

12. Repeat steps 3 through 11 for each of the other layers, in summary:

    a.   Select the next darkest layer.

    b.   Drag it to the top, making it the uppermost layer.

    c.   Add a hide-all layer mask.

    d.   Select the layer directly below.

    e.   Create the luminosity mask using the RGB channel.

    f.Return to the layer mask on the uppermost layer and paint.

13. Eventually you will have something that looks like this:

14. Notice how each layer above the next is a darker exposure and has fewer areas brushed in (brushed-in areas are white). I find that by the time I get to the windows I may be intersecting the

highlight selection (step 8) up to ten times (or more), so very little of that is brushed in.

15. Lastly, you just flatten this image, just like you would during the post processing of interior photos (Layer >> Flatten Image).

Now that you have flattened the image you have a single layer that has a broader dynamic range than any of the single images. Before going back to Lightroom, you can do other edits with this first.

Photoshop Edits

Workflows in this chapter include a step called "Photoshop Edits", so like I did with Exposure Blending, I dedicated a section here that you can refer to instead of cluttering-up the steps in each workflow.

Whether before saving your exposure-blended image to Lightroom, or at the final step when a TIFF is created (near the end of the workflows in this chapter), there are edits you can do to improve your 360 pano. Here are a few Photoshop edits I do often.

Remove camera from mirrors

A portable 360 camera on a light stand is easy to remove using the clone tool or Spot Healing Brush tool. This is usually best removed before stitching since that process can widen the camera, making it harder to edit later in the workflow.

Color Layers

Since you're not able to use flash, you will no doubt get color casts and odd white balances from portable 360 cameras, and sometimes things are off a bit when using a DSLR as well.

Adjusting the white balance in Lightroom isn't always an ideal option since it's a global adjustment, which doesn't always work well on a 360 pano covering a massive area with inevitably different white balances throughout the scene. Instead, you can *selectively* correct colors in one of two ways: Color Layers, or Selective White Balance, which I'll cover next.

For color layers, the process involves selecting an acceptable color; making a fill layer with that color; and with that layer in "color" blending mode, painting on its layer mask where you want colors to be corrected. Take for instance this image that was exposure blended:

On the far left the wall color is orange, near the fireplace it has green cast, and by the chandelier there is orange, yet under the staircase there is a more correct gray. To make colors more even, use the color picker and click on the most correct, color; in this case, below the staircase.

Now make a fill layer by selecting from the menu Layer >> New Fill Layer >> Solid Color. This will prompt you to name the layer; just hit enter. Then it shows the color picker dialog again with the color we just selected as default; click OK.

Next, set this layer's blending mode to "Color". It should now look like this:

Now invert the layer mask. You can do this by clicking on the layer mask, and then typing CTRL+I. This should turn the layer mask black (a hide-all layer mask). Now you can paint the walls. A safe way to do that is to draw a polygon around the walls you want to paint, and then with the layer mask selected using a low flow brush (10-30% flow), paint in those selected areas, like so:

Continued to paint/erase (with the mask selected) and play with the layer's fill setting until you have colors where you want and to what degree. You can also change the color at any time by double clicking the color icon on that fill layer, which will bring up the color selection dialog; in fact, if you look closely between the last two screenshots you'll see that I changed the color for our fill layer (from gray to tan).

Working with fisheye images makes it hard to draw polygonal areas for selective editing like this, so sometimes the quick selection tool works well. In any case, I often overlap onto the ceiling since I'll desaturate it later — something I'll cover shortly.

Selective White Balance

Similar to using color layers, you can also do selective white balance in Photoshop by using duplicate layers of the image; selecting a different white balance using the Camera Raw Filter tool; adding a mask to that layer; and painting where you'd like (with the layer mask selected). If you've never set white balance with Camera Raw Filter in Photoshop, it's under Filter >> Camera Raw Filter. That will bring up the Camera Raw dialog, which looks like this.

I placed an arrow pointing to the white balance dropper, which can be helpful for clicking on a neutral color in the image to help determine the white balance.

Be sure to make a duplicate layer for each white balance area you want to edit; make the white balance adjustment in Camera Raw; hide the layer with a hide-all layer mask; select the layer mask; and then paint where you desire.

Desaturate Ceilings

I like to slightly desaturate white ceilings, even in my regular interior real estate photography. These ceilings tend to be collectors of color cast, so taking away some saturation is usually a good thing. Taking our last example, here's how it's done.

First, select the ceiling, like so:

You can use Polygon, Quick Select, or other tools to select the ceiling. Don't worry about not getting too accurate as you can refine this later.

Go to the uppermost layer (in this case it was our color layer for the walls), then make a new saturation adjustment layer: Layer >> New Adjustment Layer >> Hue/Saturation and name it to whatever you'd like. You'll then have a saturation layer created with a layer mask of the areas you selected (the ceiling). Then lower the saturation slider, like so:

Note the layer mask on the saturation layer is white where we selected the ceiling. You can paint, erase, etc. from this mask to refine the area to desaturate, and also adjust the amount of desaturation with the saturation slider.

Stitching

Each portable 360 camera manufacturer takes a different approach to stitching their images with their specific software, which I touched on in the "Stitchers for Portable Cameras" section in the "Software" chapter, showing how to setup these programs (if needed), and prepare them for use. But using these stitchers in the pro editing workflow can be tedious and frustrating, especially since each is different — not only in *how* they are used, but also *when* they can be used, and with what file formats. Since stitching varies so widely across the various portable 360 cameras — it doesn't vary with DSLRs and is often simpler — I would suggest reviewing the "Stitchers for Portable Cameras" section in the "Software" chapter if you haven't done so already before moving on to the workflow steps.

Workflow Steps

Since each portable camera manufacturer has different stitching software and slightly different ways of doing things, there are differences to the steps in the workflows. In this section I outlined steps I've found useful for using the Ricoh Theta Z1, QooCam 8K, and Insta360 One X. These steps assume you know how to use Lightroom and Photoshop to some degree, and you have your camera's stitching software installed and ready to go, as outlined in the "Stitchers for Portable Cameras" section in the "Software" chapter. Additionally, presets for these workflows are in the "Lightroom Presets" chapter near the end of this book.

Ricoh Theta Z1

The workflow for the Theta Z1 is much more straightforward than the QooCam 8K and Insta360 One X steps. The Z1 is the closest to pro quality among the portable cameras I've researched, bought, and tested, and its workflow is similarly more pro oriented. Still, there are some special steps involved to get decent quality, namely because:

- You need to exposure-blend images to reduce noise and expand the dynamic range.

- Lightroom editing alone may not be enough.

- And very importantly, Ricoh's stitching software does a poor job at generating JPGs, and is notorious for color banding. Since I don't recommend Ricoh's software for generating JPGS, I recommend you work mostly with TIFFs and then use Photoshop to make your final JPGs.

Even with these nits, the Ricoh Theta Z1 workflow is the easiest of the portable cameras in this chapter. Here are the steps I recommend:

1. Import all DNGs into Lightroom and sort them by filename. This is the same as you would do for other Lightroom imports I show in my other books:

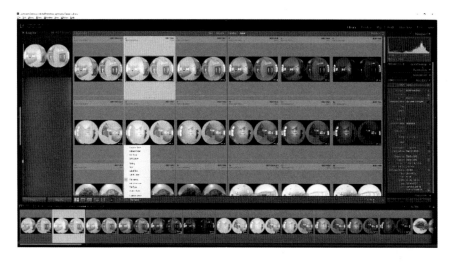

   a. Note that you can apply the import preset on import, although I prefer to do this after import. If you apply the import preset on import than you can skip to step 7

2. Go to Develop mode and select the first image.

3. Apply the import preset to one image.

4. Copy the development settings (right click on the image, then "Develop Settings" "Copy Settings") and copy all but the white balance.

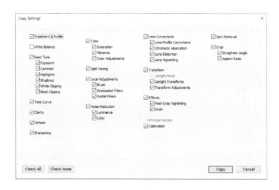

5. Select all images: Edit >> Select All, or CTRL-A.

6. Paste the development settings to all images: Right click on the images in the filmstrip and select "Development Settings" "Paste Settings".

    a. CTRL-D will then deselect the images.

7. Now go through each of your panos and perform exposure blending as shown in the "Exposure Blending" section of this chapter.

8. After exposure blending in Photoshop you can now apply other edits if you'd like, some of which I show in the "Photoshop Edits" section earlier in this chapter.

9. In Photoshop, flatten and save this file (just like you would for regular interior work) and go back to Lightroom where it should be now loaded.

10. Apply the final preset (I called it "360 Full Bump" in the presets chapter).

11. Make final adjustments using sliders and such.

12. Export as TIFF, using these settings:

13. The Ricoh Stitcher should launch once Lightroom finishes its export.

14. Click OK in the Ricoh Stitcher dialog, which will make a stitched TIFF. (See more info on the Ricoh Stitcher in the "Ricoh" section of the "Software" chapter).

15. Load this stitched TIFF into Photoshop.

16. Perform any other edits you'd like.

17. Save as a JPG from Photoshop. This JPG is what you will host later.

QooCam 8K

The QooCam workflow is similar to the Ricoh Theta Z1's but with a few inconvenient steps to overcome its limited stitching software, making this workflow more of a kludge — but doable. As you may recall from the "Software" chapter, QooCam's stitching software (QooCam Studio) isn't that great; it can't even load RAW files shot with their own camera. To make their software work with the maximum editing flexibility in the workflows, I recommend using the QooCam Studio software as the very last step, loading a TIFF file to be stitched; however, QooCam Studio expects the image orientation to be as it was taken out of the camera — vertical. So to make editing easier, this requires rotation at two different times in the workflow steps. Here are the steps (as painful as they may be) that I recommend for the QooCam 8K:

1. Import all DNGs into Lightroom and sort them by filename. This is the same as you would do for other Lightroom imports I show in my other books (and in the last workflow for the Ricoh Theta Z1 as well).

   a. You can apply the import preset on import, although I prefer to do this after import. If you apply the import preset on import than you can skip to step 7.

2. Go to Develop mode and select the first image.

3. Apply the import preset to one image.

4. Copy the development settings (right click on the image, then "Develop Settings" "Copy Settings") and copy all but the white balance.

5. Select all images: Edit >> Select All, or CTRL-A.

6. Paste the development settings to all images: Right click on the images in the filmstrip and select "Development Settings" "Paste Settings".

   a. CTRL-D will then deselect the images.

7. Now go through each of your panos, loading the layers into Photoshop to perform exposure blending as shown in the "Exposure Blending" section of this chapter.

   a. To make this step easier, it's best to rotate this entire image 90° clockwise as QooCam Studio requires their images be in portrait orientation, not landscape. Landscape orientation is easier to work with on a monitor, so now would the time to rotate 90° clockwise. We'll rotate that back later.

8. After exposure blending in Photoshop you can now apply other edits if you'd like, some of which I show in the "Photoshop Edits" section earlier in this chapter.

9. Flatten and save this file (just like you would for regular interior work) and go back to Lightroom, where it should be now loaded.

10. Apply the final preset (360 Full Bump).

11. Make any final adjustments with sliders and such.

12. If you rotated your image 90° in step 7.a, then it's time to rotate it back 90° the other direction (counterclockwise).

13. Export as TIFF. You don't have to be as strict about where to export to, or what to name the file as you would with the Ricoh. But, you do need to make sure you include all Metadata.

14. Launch QooCam Studio.

15. Load the TIFF into QooCam Studio.

16. Render as JPG. This JPG is what you will host later.

Insta360 One X

The Insta360 Studio software can't load a TIFF file, only JPGs or DNG RAW files. This complicates the workflow as you can't stitch a TIFF at the very end like you would with the Ricoh and QooCam. Instead, you can either stitch all of your DNG files and then edit them as layers using Lightroom and Photoshop, or a simpler approach is to use PTGui as the stitching program at the very end of the workflow, which allows you to load a TIFF file for stitching. I'll be using the PTGui option for this workflow.

1. Import all of the DNGs into Lightroom and sort them by filename. This is the same as you would do for other Lightroom imports I show in my other books (and in the earlier workflows for the Ricoh Theta Z1 and QooCam).

    a. You can apply the import preset on import, although I prefer to do this after import. If you apply the import preset on import than you can skip to step 7

2. Go to Develop mode and select the first image.

3. Apply the import preset to one image.

4. Copy the development settings (right click on the image, then "Develop Settings" "Copy Settings") and copy all but the white balance.

5. Select all images: Edit >> Select All, or CTRL-A.

6. Paste the development settings to all images: Right click on the images in the filmstrip and select "Development Settings" "Paste Settings".

    a. CTRL-D will then deselect the images.

7. Now go through each of your panos, loading the layers into Photoshop to perform exposure blending as shown in the "Exposure Blending" section of this chapter.

   a. To make this step easier, it is best to rotate this entire image 90° clockwise, as Insta360 Studio requires their images be in portrait orientation, not landscape, which is easier to work with on a monitor.

8. After exposure blending in Photoshop you can now apply other edits if you'd like, some of which I show in the "Photoshop Edit" section earlier in this chapter.

9. Flatten and save this file (just like you would for regular interior work) and go back to Lightroom, where it should be now loaded.

10. Apply the final preset (360 Full Bump).

11. Make any final adjustments with sliders and such.

12. If you rotated your image 90° in step 7.a, then it's time to rotate it back 90° the other direction (counterclockwise).

13. Export as TIFF, and make sure to include all Metadata.

14. Launch PTGui, and follow the steps in the next chapter, "PTGui Primer", loading the TIFF you exported from Lightroom.

   a. In the create panorama step, you can save this as a JPG, or you could export as a TIFF and do further editing in Photoshop, and then save that as a JPG. The JPG is what you will host later.

Nadir Patching

If you're like me and don't shoot the nadir (most of the time anyways), then you can apply a patch. You can do the same patch that I'll show shortly for nadir patching DSLR 360 panos, or you might be able to clone, or otherwise edit out your light stand from your finished 360 pano. This is easier to do with portable 360 camera panos (before stitching) since the DSLR method has a bigger footprint below the camera (a tripod versus a light stand). I find though that the tiny light stand in the nadir of portable 360 camera panos is so small that I just don't bother with it, and I haven't had a client complain yet — many in fact, get a kick out of it since it looks like a tiny robot.

DSLR Workflow

The workflow for DSLR cameras can be easier than those for portable 360 cameras. If you're already shooting interior real estate than it's a workflow you'll likely be familiar with as well. Nevertheless, even though things become more streamlined in the DSLR workflow, it can be more complicated at times. While that may seem counterintuitive, remember that since you're using a DSLR to capture images, you don't have to fiddle around with proprietary stitching software to create your 360 pano; instead, you'll use a universal stitching program, like PTGui, which I'll use for the workflow here. Using PTGui is where things may get tricky, but if you shoot your panos properly then things usually go quick and easy.

When it comes to the DSLR workflow you can optionally use flash for interior work, including the flash-ambient blending and window pull techniques I cover in my earlier books, and which I also discussed earlier in this book in the "Using Flash" chapter. You can do much more editing than portable cameras allow since you can push DSLR images further in post processing; however, the key is to make sure you use minimal processing before stitching, and then edit mostly with *global* edits once fully stitched. The operative word here is "global", since it's important to have as much consistency as possible in your pano as it spins around. This is especially important on each side since it will wrap into itself, and any differences between those two sides can create lines showing the edit differences.

Here are the steps that I recommend for the DSLR workflow:

1. Import all of our RAW files into Lightroom and sort them by filename, just like you would any other real estate project (like I show in the interiors book).

    a. You can apply the import preset on import, although I prefer to do this after import. If you apply the import preset on import than you can skip to step 7.

2. Go to Develop mode and select the first image.

3. Apply the import preset (shown in the "Presets" chapter) to the first image. This is a basic preset that, like presets for the 360 cameras, has zero sharpening, and only "Remove Chromatic Aberrations" selected. **DO NOT DO ANY LENS CORRECTION**.

4. Copy the development settings (right click on the image, then "Develop Settings" "Copy Settings") and copy all but the white balance.

5. Select all images: Edit >> Select All, or CTRL-A.

6. Paste the development settings to all images: Right click on the images in the filmstrip and select "Development Settings" "Paste Settings".

    a. CTRL-D will then deselect the images.

7. If you are not using flash, then skip to step 10. Otherwise, if you are using flash, then flash-ambient blend your footage in Photoshop like I show in the "Using Flash" chapter. In short, this involves:

    a. Loading your images as layers in Photoshop.

b. Ensure ambient shot is the top layer.

c. Set the ambient layer's blending mode to Luminosity.

d. Set the ambient layer's opacity to 60% or 70%, making sure to use this same percentage on all of the images (all four rotation shots, zenith, and optional nadir).

8. Add optional window pulls (also covered in the "Using Flash" chapter). Similar to other edits across images for a 360 pano, it's important that the window pulls be consistent, shot at the same exposure. Because of this, I try to setup my shots so that the primary view window does not overlap into other images. That can't always be the case, but as long as you shoot each window pull at the same exposure, then this shouldn't be a problem in the stitching process.

9. Flatten and save the image, which will load it back into Lightroom.

10. Export this image as a 16-bit TIFF. Ensure that "All Metadata" is selected. Your export window should look something like this:

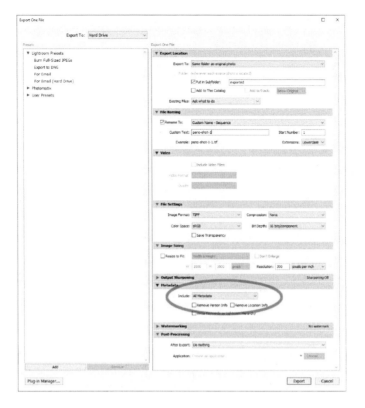

11. Repeat steps 7 through 10 for the other three rotational shots and the zenith shot as well (nadir also if you shot it).

    a. If you're not using flash then this means you'll just keep exporting the images you want from Lightroom (step 10).

12. Load these TIFFs into PTGui for stitching (the four rotation, zenith, and optional nadir shots). I included detailed instructions for doing this in the next chapter ("PTGui Primer") under the "Basic Stitching" section. While that section will drill into the detailed steps (and also why), the basic steps using PTGui are:

    a. Align images.

    b. Fix control points if necessary.

c. Create panorama, using TIFF format, 16 bits, no compression.

13. Load that stitched TIFF into Photoshop to apply the final edits.

14. In Photoshop, duplicate the layer of your TIFF file. This duplicated layer is where you will apply your edits in the next steps, thus providing a non-destructive means for editing.

   a. Side Note: If you encounter any strange stitching lines when the 360 pano is rendered by your 360 host (covered in the next chapter), this is often caused by editing. All you have to do is go back to Photoshop, apply a mask to the duplicated/edited layer, and erase where the lines are showing up in rendering. Thus, it's important to duplicate the layer and save the two layers in a PSD file to edit later if need be.

15. On the duplicated layer, you can apply one of your Lightroom presets using Adobe Camera Raw. In Photoshop this is located in the menus at Filter >> Camera Raw Filter, and then select the presets tab on the top right. Here's a partial screenshot showing me applying one of my interior presets (this shows presets you created in Lightroom). See presets for Interiors and Exteriors in the "Lightroom Presets" chapter near the end of this book:

16. With the Camera Raw window still open, you can make other adjustments and edits as well, perhaps tweaking the white balance and other sliders in the "Basic" pane. It's not recommended to get too fancy with Photoshop layers; instead, applying "global" edits using sliders and such with Adobe Camera Raw (like you would with Lightroom) will lower the risk of odd rendering issues when you upload your final image to your 360 host.

17. Lastly, save this as a JPG. This is your final image, ready to upload to your 360 host.

Nadir Patching

If you didn't take a nadir shot for your 360 pano, then you might want to add a quick patch. There are a number of ways to patch your nadir in the DSLR workflow, including:

1. Do a content-aware fill in Photoshop after the 360 pano has been stitched.

2. Add a nadir patch.

Sometimes I do option #1, which is no different than any other content-aware fill you'd do in Photoshop. I like option #2 the best though, which gives you a nadir like in this example 360 pano:

virtual-tour-book.remotehomeshowings.com/nadir-patch

Here are the steps to make this patch using Photoshop:

1. Create a new file in Photoshop. Usually 4000 x 4000 pixels works well, with a black background, 300 pixels per inch, RGB Color 16 bit.

2. Using the text tool, color white, and large font, type something like this:

3. Flatten the image: Layer >> Flatten Image

4. Go to Filter >> Distort >> Polar Coordinates and make sure "Polar to Rectangular" is selected and press OK.

5. You should now see something like this:

6. Go to Image >> Image Rotation >> Flip Canvas Vertically

7. Go to Image >> Image Rotation >> Flip Canvas Horizontally

8. You should now see something like this:

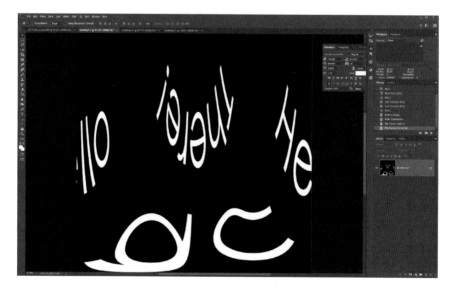

9. From the menus: Select >> All (or CTRL-A).

10. Copy this: CTRL-C.

11. Open your 360 pano in Photoshop and paste this: CTRL-V. You should see something like this:

12. Now use Edit >> Transform >> Scale to resize this image over the blank nadir area. In this example the nadir is all white at the bottom. Once you have it scaled properly over this area, if should look like this:

13. Now just save the file as a JPG like you normally would. Once it is hosted as a 360 pano, you'll see something that looks like this:

If you are shooting for a commercial client, this is a great place to put their logo.

Another, simpler option is to just make a blank, black layer without the text and do the same steps for scaling it in place. That will leave a black circle with no text.

PTGui Primer

PTGui (ptgui.com) is mainly used for stitching 360 panos shot with a DSLR. It can also be useful for portable 360° cameras since PTGui is a *universal* stitching program. If you are shooting 360 panos with a DSLR though, you will need PTGui or a similar program. Like most everything in the world of photography, anything powerful that produces high quality results can seem complicated at first. But I believe the learning curve for PTGui is short and well worth the time. By learning some of PTGui's basics you can open a world of possibilities for processing your 360 panos.

PTGui has a series of video tutorials, which can help bring you up to speed very quickly at:

ptgui.com/videotutorials.html

I highly recommend these free videos. In this chapter I'll merely scratch the surface of the more salient features I found useful in PTGui for making 360 panos for real estate virtual tours. This isn't an exhaustive list, but simply things I use most often with PTGui.

Basic Stitching

The simplest way to use PTGui is to use its Project Assistant, which provides a 3-step process to make a 360 pano. If you shot your pano properly, then this 3-stop process goes quick. The first step is to just open or drag your images to the application, like so:

In this example I dragged 5 images (TIFF files) onto PTGui, which PTGui loaded under step #1 (Source images). These were the four rotational shots at 90° each, and one zenith shot (pointing the camera straight up). I didn't include a nadir, which as I mentioned earlier in the book, I usually don't bother with.

Next, click the "Align images" button. If all goes well (something I'll get to next if it doesn't) PTGui should stitch a 360 pano and display an additional window called the "Panorama Editor" like this:

By not shooting the nadir I'm left with a black area on the bottom of the pano. That's not a big deal for most of my real estate work as there are a number of ways to deal with that later if I want, including the patching I showed in the "Nadir Patching" section in the DSLR Workflow.

You can edit the pano further in this window, but I find most of the time I can just close it. Going back to the main window, go to step #3 and click the "Create panorama" button, which will change to the Create Panorama screen here:

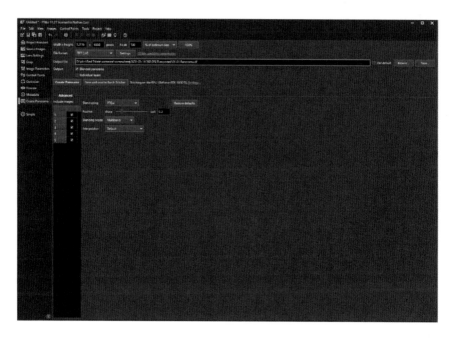

On this screen you enter the info to generate the 360 pano image. This defaults to JPG but I recommend you output it as a 16-bit TIFF, like I showed in the screenshot above. And then click the "Create Panorama" button on this screen.

That's it! You should now have a 360 pano, which you can load into Photoshop and apply edits (more on that in the DSLR workflow in the "Editing Workflows" chapter).

These 3 simple steps assume that everything was ideally shot for PTGui, but that's not always the case. Sometimes after aligning images you might get this error:

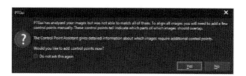

This is where things get a little tricky. Let's cover that next.

Control Points

PTGui stitches your images automatically by detecting common points that overlap across the images. These are known as "Control Points", which sometimes need a little help using PTGui's Control Point editor. If something went wrong aligning images, you may get an error from PTGui complaining about these control points. In such a case, all you need to do is go to the Control Points screen, shown below and define some control points for PTGui to use:

Each side of the Control Points screen shows an image and the control points they share. In this example I'm looking at image #2 on the left and image #3 on the right. The colored number boxes show the various control points — the common points PTGui will use to line up these images when it does its stitching. Well-overlapped images provide better/more control points, which is why you want to shoot four vertical/portrait-oriented shots at 90° and a zenith. But while your four rotation shots and zenith can overlap nicely most of the time, PTGui is searching for points in high contrast areas; thus, if you were to shoot an empty room with the ceiling color the same as the walls, PTGui may struggle to find high contrast regions to define its control points. The zenith shot can be an issue in itself since most ceilings are featureless, and thus harder to find control points to use. Take this next screen shot for example:

Here I'm looking at shot #1 on the left and shot #5 (the zenith) on the right. There are no control points, since the ceiling in image 1 is fairly featureless. This, btw, is something to consider when composing your pano: try to ensure that your zenith will include some kind of contrasted area (ceiling corners, ceiling lights, smoke detectors, window or door frames, etc.) that will also be present in some of the four rotational shots. Putting your tripod at a reasonable height usually solves this since putting your camera too high might not capture a room's corners in the zenith shot. In this particular example, even though there were no control points between images #1 and the zenith (image #5), some of the other images had features overlapping with the zenith, shown below:

Other images were able to utilize the hanging lamp, but even in this case PTGui was only able to find control points in two places (the doorbell ringer and a corner cut-out). I could add more control points, which is something you have to do if PTGui throws an error on the align process. It's simple to do, like so:

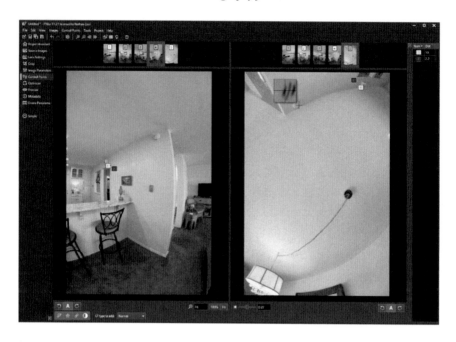

Here I placed my cursor, using my mouse, on a spot over the smoke detector on image #5 (on the right). PTGui automatically found the corresponding point on image #4 (note the crosshairs on the smoke detector). If though it couldn't find its corresponding point on the other image, you just move your mouse/cursor to that spot and give it a click. You can also bring up a table of all control points across all images by clicking the table icon in the Control Points screen, shown below:

You can double click an entry in this table and PTGui will load the two corresponding images with that control point selected. The "Distance" column is the most critical info in this table as it will show poor control points that may need your attention: the higher the distance, the poorer the quality of the control point pair.

Once you've improved the control points, the next step would be to run the Optimizer. Just go to the Optimizer screen and click the "Run Optimizer" button, which will give you results, like this shown below:

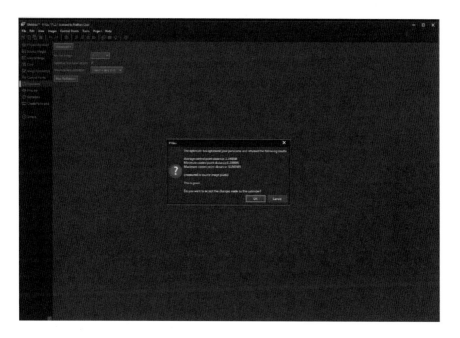

In this case my pano stitching was rated as good. Hurray! Now you can go back to the Project Assistant screen and finish with step 3 (Create panorama). If you want to see the results before you do, just bring up the Panorama Editor window (under the Tools menu).

Output

To maximize stitching efficiency and editing quality, I recommend that you don't do any major post processing of your input images; instead, wait until you output your pano from PTGui (as a TIFF) and then do your final edits in Photoshop with this stitched TIFF. I like to edit the stitched TIFF with Camera Raw in Photoshop as that tool can apply my Lightroom presets; something I talk about more in the "Editing Workflows" chapter, in particular in the "DSLR Workflow" section, and I can do other edits in Photoshop with adjustment layers and such with more flexibility than using Lightroom alone.

Hosting

Once you created your 360 panos it's time to put them somewhere people can view them. New 360 hosting services pop up regularly, some of which I covered in the "Hosting Services" chapter. Here I'll discuss the steps for hosting your panos in a virtual tour. Since each 360 virtual tour hosting provider is similar, and quite simple to use, I'll keep this chapter as generic as possible, but with a concentration on my two recommendations from earlier: Cloudpano and Marzipano.

Uploading

Uploading your 360 panos to your host is usually as simple as drag-and-drop. With Cloudpano you just click the "Add Images" button and drag and drop your 360 panos onto their pop-up window:

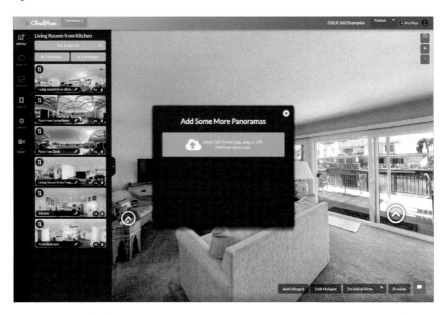

Marzipano has a similar pop-up window when it starts, but then to add more panoramas you have to click the "Add more panoramas" button, which brings up a file dialog where you have to navigate to where your other panos are located.

Note that Marzipano may throw an error if the aspect ratio of a pano is not 2:1; most 360 panos have that ratio so it's a rare error. If you do get an error it's an easy fix using PTGui, but something to be aware of: In PTGui's Panorama Editor go the Projection menu and select "Spherical 360° X 180°" and it will crop the image by leaving extra space in the nadir. You can then use the techniques I mentioned earlier concerning nadir patching to deal with that blank space.

Once your panos are uploaded, you can change their names (which default to the file name). You can usually also drag them up or down on the list on the left to order them. Here's a screen shot of Marzipano with those options:

You set the title of the tour in Marzipano by editing where it says "Project Title" near the top left.

Setting the Initial View

Each pano needs to have its initial view set by you: the initial view a user sees when they select a pano/scene. The default is often not where you want your view to start, so setting this is important. Setting it is easy: just spin your pano to where you want it to start, and then click the "Set Initial View" button. See also "Initial View Optimization" in the "Photographing a 360" chapter for how to compose for this when you shoot your pano.

Adding Navigation

Once you have all of your 360 panos uploaded for your tour, it's time to add navigation arrows and optional info icons. These are known as "Link hotspots" and "Info hotspots". Link hotspots link panos/scenes so you can click and move to that scene, and Info hotspots provide pop-up windows with additional info, and in some cases images as well.

Link hotspots are the most critical, but you need to have all of your panos uploaded first so that all of those panos can link to each other when you add those hotspots. Here's a screenshot of Cloudpano's Link hotspot pop-up:

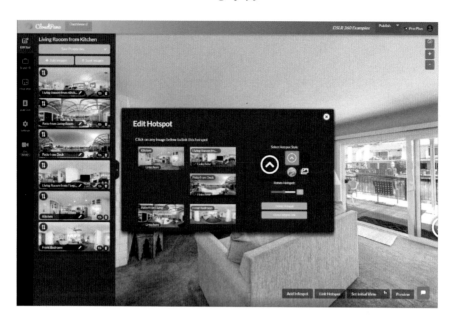

This is a fairly intuitive dialog, whereas Marzipano, while actually being more flexible in some regards, is a tiny little window gizmo that you have to move around to position where you want the hotspot:

This small pop-up shows the list of panos/scenes you can link the hotspot to. Cloudpano does this smarter by showing you scenes that are linked to the scene you are working on, making it much more intuitive and less prone to selecting the wrong scene.

Make sure that every scene has at least one entry and exit point. You don't want someone to enter a room and not be able to leave.

Publishing

The last step in hosting a virtual tour is to publish it. This is usually as simple as just clicking a "Publish" button, which gives you a link you can share (and for realtors to use in their MLS listing). This is different though if self-publishing, like using Marzipano.

Marzipano has an "Export" button on the top right of their screen, which will create a zip file that is downloaded onto your computer. You can then upload those files to your web server, and edit the web files if you want to brand it some special way. As mentioned earlier, self-hosting requires some level of web tech knowledge.

Note that you can also self-publish a tour with Cloudpano. Under their "Publish" button, they have an option "Download and host on your own server". This provides files, similar to Marzipano, which you can upload to your web server and change as needed.

Embedding

If you have web tech experience and you want to embed your virtual tour in a web page, know that most 360 hosts provide you with embed code, similar to this from Cloudpano:

```
<iframe id="/tours/12345"
allow="vr;accelerometer;gyroscope;fullscreen"
allowfullscreen frameborder="0" width="100%" height="500"
src="https://app.cloudpano.com/tours/12345"></iframe>
```

The "12345" is your tour number, which you could assign as a variable, for instance if using PHP or similar language, thus making your tours more scalable/portable.

Pricing

In this chapter I want to briefly discuss how you might establish a pricing structure for your virtual tours. This builds somewhat on pricing covered in my book on business techniques, although this chapter is geared toward virtual tours, depending on the methods you choose.

As with other real estate photography, virtual tour pricing varies widely based on geography, expertise, quality, and client. But unlike other real estate photography work, virtual tour pricing is also affected by legacy technology as things are changing rapidly in this field yet some clients base their expectations on older ways of doing business. This is similar to the advent of drone photography when legacy tech, using a helicopter, could easily cost $500/hour, thus costing a client $1,000 (or more) to get a full set of aerial photos. But when drones became more readily available, a wide range of prices emerged. Even today you'll find drone photographers charging anywhere from $50 to $500 for a basic shoot. The former won't likely be experienced (or licensed) while the latter will likely provide a higher end product. Yet while drone photography was supplanting helicopter aerial work, not only were prices shifting, but the offerings were changing as well. With a drone, for instance, you can do things a helicopter can't: fly through a backyard, fly into or up to a house, etc. So it wasn't just a change in technology that shifted aerial photography pricing; it was newer creative options that set others apart, thus driving prices for various markets and clientele. The field of virtual tours is facing a similar shift today.

Lower cost tech with more options for higher quality products and hosting has widened the field of virtual tour photography, making pricing all the more difficult. For instance, if you do a web search for virtual tour pricing, you'll likely find virtual tour pricing ranging anywhere from $100 to $1000. This wide gap differs not just on property size, but also the type of work needed, the quality, and legacy pricing structures. While the $100 offerings are usually just teaser, "starting" prices from lower quality tour companies, many virtual tours for real estate listings in the past ran about $0.10 to $0.15 per square foot, with a minimum price usually based on a 2,500 square foot home; hence, *starting* prices were, in the past, often as low as $250 to $375 for many markets in the U.S. Those were often starting prices, with, for instance, 5,000 square foot homes running upwards of $500 to $750 in some markets. Lower priced tours (the "starting at $100" teasers) that competed with those kinds of prices often limited tour hosting to a few months; required add-ons for anything beyond just a basic tour; and were most always very low quality tours. With this wide spread of options it may seem like prices are a moving target, but there are simple ways to calculate your pricing structure.

First, due-diligence on your part is crucial to understanding current price expectations in your area. However, it, like any other price structure research, should not be the only factor or a deterrent. Instead, *effort* is the key component for establishing modern virtual tour pricing, knowing what your market supports now and offerings you can provide that perhaps were never (or rarely) done before. For instance, providing virtual tours for businesses tends to have a higher price tag than real estate listings, which reflects the amount of effort and hence quality of the virtual tour, since businesses often want a one-time, high quality tour that would most likely be shot with a DSLR. For real estate listings though, virtual tours are often quick-turn, temporary media assets that will no longer be used once a property is sold; hence, quality expectations are often lower, which is reflected in the price. However, some real estate listings require (or desire) the highest quality virtual tour possible, such as oceanfront/waterfront properties, or similar listings where inside-outside property views and stellar imaging overall drives a higher selling price. These variables could make it difficult to decide what to charge your clients for virtual tours, but if you're already doing real estate photography and have prices established for standard real estate photography work, then you can convert that into pricing for virtual tours by establishing your base rate, and then calculating an added effort for the work required. That's the approach I'll address in this chapter.

As I mentioned earlier in the book, you don't have to choose either portable 360 cameras or DSLRs for shooting virtual tours. You can use both, allowing you to create flexible pricing for various levels of work. For instance, I offer a basic package that uses just a portable 360 camera; another package (called the Impact package) with up to five DSLR shots and the remainder with a portable 360 camera; and yet another (called the Ultimate) with all DSLR shots. For businesses, you can quote by the job using hourly rate calculations, similar to those in my business techniques book. Here though I'd like to concentrate on a pricing example by establishing a 3-offering structure that uses:

- All portable 360 camera

  o You might name this offering "Basic".

- Mix of DSLR and portable 360 camera

  o You could name this "Luxury". I call mine Impact.

- All DSLR camera

  o You could name this "Luxury Deluxe", or similar. I call mine "Ultimate".

Aside from what you want to call these offerings/packages, the first variable to establish in calculating these offerings is your base rate (Br). When it comes to 360 virtual tours, especially if you're self-hosting or using something budget-friendly like Cloudpano, you could set your base rate the same as what you charge for one of your standard photoshoots. For instance, if you provide 12 scenes for a virtual tour using a portable 360 camera (common for homes under 3,000 square feet) then the price could be the same as a standard photoshoot for that same size of home. Thus, your base rate would be:

- Br = photoshoot price for size of home

Br, once again, would be for using a portable 360 camera only. This should compensate you for the time on site (which is fairly low), and the editing time (which can be high using a portable 360 camera). You can further that base rate according to your other standard pricing tiers; for instance, if you price based on square footage then you might have Br1 for up to 3,000 square feet, Br2 for the next tier, perhaps up to 4,000 square feet, etc., each of which would deliver more scenes. Similarly, if you charge by the number of photos for your standard photoshoots, then you would establish Br1, Br2, etc. based on those *quantity* tiers, since each virtual tour would also likely have more scenes. Here though I'll just use Br for the rest of the calculations.

Once you have established your base rate (Br), then you can establish the feature-based tier pricing. In this case let's use Basic, Impact, and Ultimate, where P = price.

- Basic: All scenes shot with a portable 360 camera.

  o P = Br

- Impact: Up to five scenes shot with a DSLR (main living areas, kitchen, master bed/bath, and backyard), remainder of the scenes shot with a portable 360 camera. Since the DSLR shots will comprise almost half of the total scenes (typical 12 total scenes for standard sized homes) yet could take more effort, you can establish its price as:

  o P = Br + (Br * 0.5)

- Ultimate: All scenes shot with a DSLR, basically double the effort and hence cost.

  o P = Br * 2

For example, let's say that for a standard photoshoot for a home up to 3,000 square feet you charge $300. A basic tour would then be priced at $300; Impact would be priced at $450; and Ultimate would be priced at $600.

Another way to calculate your pricing structure is to use base price plus price-per-square-footage, which has been common with virtual tour pricing in the past. For instance, you could charge a base price of your hourly rate; let's say that's $150. Then you could add $0.10 per square foot. For a 3,000 square foot home, that comes out to:

- $150 + (3,000 * $0.10) = $450

This though might assume you will shoot an unlimited number of scenes, and it doesn't take into account your efforts of using either portable cameras or DSLRs. But, you could do a hybrid pricing approach where certain sizes of homes get different levels of attention, and thus pricing.

The main problem you may face with pricing today is what clients may already be accustomed to and quotes they get from your competitors. Since Matterport has been around longer than most of the newer services and cameras, its inherently stringent, single way of shooting and delivering tours fits within a single-feature pricing structure based almost entirely on property size. Since you don't have flexibility in shooting and editing with Matterport like you would with other 360 services and cameras, their pricing was as simple as their product: you get one kind of product for one kind of price. But with the virtual tour market now expanding with new cameras, hosts, and services, a one-size-fits-all pricing structure would not be one that grows with this quickly evolving field.

The next step in establishing your pricing is to do research for your area, just as you would when establishing pricing for your other work. Similarly, don't just use someone else's prices; instead, charge what you are worth, and what your market can support, commensurate with your effort. If your clients are entirely happy with virtual tours shot with a portable 360 camera, then price your services accordingly. If you have luxury clients that weren't keen on virtual tours in the past because of quality but now you can wow them with DSLR panos using flash, then perhaps provide a luxury pricing package for those clients as well. No matter what route you take for pricing, remember to know your market, give them what they want but at prices commensurate with your effort, while continually looking for higher roads that lead to higher levels of your success.

Further Reading

I hope you enjoyed this seventh book in my real estate photography series, and that you can use some of these techniques in your photography as well. I'd like to invite you to browse my other books on real estate photography, which I think you'll find useful to improve your skills and further your photography career. All of my books are available in paperback and e-book formats through Amazon, as well as my website, (www.NathanCoolPhoto.com).

- *Photography for Real Estate Interiors: How to take and create impressive interior photos.* From gear to editing, composition, lighting, settings, techniques and more, this is a comprehensive guide for shooting high-quality interior real estate photography from start to finish, using techniques and efficient workflow with cost-effective tools to speed up your shooting and editing processes. With numerous real-world examples, screen shots, diagrams, and external links to my video tutorials, you'll learn the principles that I and many other professional real estate photographers apply to our work.

- *Advanced Editing for Real Estate Photography: Professional techniques for processing high-quality images.* In this second book in my real estate photography series I show advanced editing techniques to create high-end real estate images. In-depth, detailed instructions are coupled with over 150 screenshots and example images to guide you step-by-step through the tools used to repair images, validate exposures, correct problematic colors and artifacts, and easily remove unwanted items. Learn how to quickly add sunny skies to cloudy days, impactful TV scenery, and natural fireplace swaps. See how simple it is to evenly light a room by putting together photo composites in post-processing, along with tricks to make showers pop and hardwood floors look rich. In this book I place an emphasis on efficiency, sharing various

Lightroom presets and showing how to turn repetitive Photoshop processes into one-button actions.

- ***Photography for Real Estate Exteriors: Taking and making professional first-impression images***. In this third book in my real estate photography series I take you step by step through the challenges to shoot and edit professional, exterior photos. With easy to understand terms, instructions and discussions, coupled with over 100 images and screenshots, this book progresses through basic- to expert-level techniques on how to master exterior composition, lighting, exposure blending, color compensation, camera settings, gear choices, distortion issues, and more. Learn how to capture and quickly edit stunning twilight photos; create impressive indoor-outdoor images; and shoot large properties using an alternative to drone photography that doesn't require FAA certification. Along with Lightroom presets included in this book — made specifically for exterior photography — you'll learn rapid workflow procedures that turn regular photos into impactful images. See how you can create curb-appealing pictures that pop, placing you in the ranks of high-end photography.

- ***Business Techniques for Real Estate Photography: How to make money shooting homes***. In this fourth book in my real estate photography series I explain how to successfully start, manage, and grow your real estate photography business. Attracting clients and keeping them for the long-term are some of the more salient themes, along with how to judge viability for your region, set prices, raise prices, and collect payments as well. By explaining aspects of human psychology that relate to clients and the industry, I show traps and scams to watch out for, and ways to deal with problem situations while maintaining the high ground. To keep you on budget I explain how to efficiently market yourself without breaking the bank, how to efficiently construct your schedule, and techniques to get your business started quickly while addressing longer term goals and growth strategies. Safety is also paramount with advice on how to stay safe on the job, and how to protect and insure your business as well. This book steers clear of hype and focuses instead on what works (and what doesn't) to create and maintain a successful real estate photography business. While the art and technical aspects of real estate photography can be challenging, doing it for money can be even more daunting. This book makes it simple though and gets right to the point, showing how you can make money shooting homes.

- ***Shot Lists for Real Estate Photography: What to shoot, and why.*** In this fifth book in my real estate photography series I take you room by room and outside as well to show an easy and efficient strategy to photographing homes. By knowing what shots and compositions will have the highest positive impact on clients and buyers, this book shows what works well, and why. With more than 200 examples you'll see numerous homes, room designs, property layouts, and photographic challenges that you can quickly identify and optimize while shooting almost any property. Along with explanations on why certain compositions are preferred over others, this book suggests image quantities for rooms and amenities in assorted home sizes, and how they relate to price-packaging tiers. Although it's suggested to be familiar with the interiors and exteriors books in my real estate photography series, the principles in "Shot Lists" show how any style of photography can apply to the shot lists, compositions, and techniques contained in this book. I also provide "Quick Pro Tips" throughout the book with easy-to-apply tricks and techniques, as well as a pre-shoot preparation checklist you can pass along to clients. Knowing not only what to shoot but also why, the photos you deliver to clients will have a higher wow-factor, proving that you aren't a consumer with a camera; but instead, you're a pro.

- ***The Lighting Guide for Real Estate Photography: How to master interior flash photography.*** In this sixth book in my real estate photography series I show techniques, setups, and options for lighting various rooms, interior spaces, and various configurations. With numerous lighting diagrams and example images, you can learn ways to light simple, intermediate, and advanced interior spaces while understanding why certain techniques are preferred over others, and under varying circumstances, so that you can apply these principles to almost any interior space you may encounter. Along with detailed information on popular lighting gear used for interior real estate photography, I discuss various lighting methods in-depth, along with tables for flash power starting points for each example, and how they differ across flash units. This lighting guide builds on techniques in my interiors book, and it's a great companion guide for my book "Shot Lists" as well. By using professional techniques for interior flash photography you can gain the know-how to tackle almost interior lighting challenge to help you show your clients that you're not just a consumer with a camera; but instead, you're a pro.

Lightroom Presets

The presets in this chapter assume you are importing either RAW files (DNG) or TIFF files, not JPGs. These presets can be used in Lightroom or the Camera Raw Filter tool in Photoshop.

Portable 360 Cameras

Since portable cameras like the Theta Z1, QooCam, and Insta360 One X are notorious for noise in the shadows, it's crucial to ensure you don't add any sharpening until the very last step in your post processing. This is done with two presets: one when you import that has no sharpening, and then one before you export your image that has a ton of sharpening, offset with a high sharpening mask and noise reduction as well. The following are the two presets I recommend for portable 360 cameras.

360 Import

Performed when importing images into Lightroom.

Section	Item	Amount
Detail	Sharpening	0
Lens Correction	Enable Profile Corrections	Unchecked
	Remove Chromatic Aberration	Checked

360 Full Bump

Performed as the very last step in post processing prior to exporting your final image. This preset is a starting point from which you can make further adjustments after applying.

Section	Item	Amount
Basic	Contrast	+15
	Highlights	-50
	Shadows	+50
	Whites	+30
	Blacks	-25
	Clarity	+22
Detail, Sharpening	Amount	100
	Radius	1.0
	Detail	25
	Masking	35
Detail, Noise Reduction	Luminance	25
	Detail	50
	Contrast	0
	Color	65
	Detail (Noise)	50
	Smoothness	50

Lens Correction	Enable Profile Corrections	Unchecked
	Remove Chromatic Aberration	Checked

DSLR

Import

Performed when importing images into Lightroom. Make sure you do NOT do any lens corrections except for removing chromatic aberration.

Section	Item	Amount
Detail	Sharpening	0
Lens Correction	Enable Profile Corrections	Unchecked
	Remove Chromatic Aberration	Checked

Interior

Usually applied in Photoshop using Adobe Camera Raw. This preset is a starting point from which you can make further adjustments after applying.

Section	Item	Amount

Basic	Contrast	+15
	Highlights	-70
	Shadows	+65
	Whites	+30
	Blacks	-4
	Clarity	+10
Detail, Sharpening	Amount	40
	Radius	1.0
	Detail	25
	Masking	40
Lens Correction	Enable Profile Corrections	Unchecked
	Remove Chromatic Aberration	Checked

Exterior

Usually applied in Photoshop using Adobe Camera Raw. This preset is a starting point from which you can make further adjustments after applying.

Section	Item	Amount
Basic	Contrast	+10
	Highlights	-40

	Shadows	+45
	Whites	+40
	Blacks	-10
	Clarity	+8
	Vibrance	+8
	Saturation	+5
Detail, Sharpening	Amount	40
	Radius	1.0
	Detail	25
	Masking	40

Made in the USA
Columbia, SC
13 August 2020